O₂
STRATFORD

ENGLAND

Avon

● STRATFORD

● OXFORD

London

Thames

English Channel

HarperCollins*Publishers*

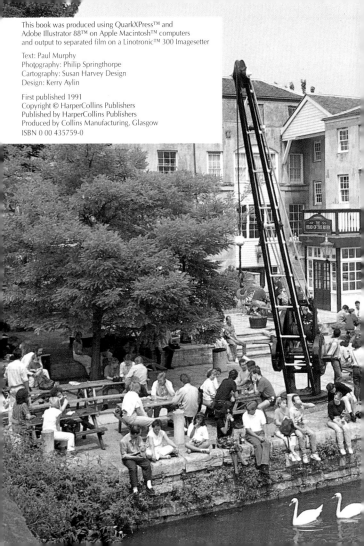

This book was produced using QuarkXPress™ and
Adobe Illustrator 88™ on Apple Macintosh™ computers
and output to separated film on a Linotronic™ 300 Imagesetter

Text: Paul Murphy
Photography: Philip Springthorpe
Cartography: Susan Harvey Design
Design: Kerry Aylin

First published 1991
Copyright © HarperCollins Publishers
Published by HarperCollins Publishers
Produced by Collins Manufacturing, Glasgow
ISBN 0 00 435759-0

HOW TO USE THIS BOOK

Your Collins Traveller Guide will help you find your way around your holiday destination quickly and easily. It is split into two sections which are colour-coded:

The blue section provides you with an alphabetical sequence of headings, from **EXCURSIONS** to **WHAT TO SEE** via **PUBS**, **RESTAURANTS**, **WALKS**, etc. in Oxford and Stratford. Each entry in a topic includes information on how to get there, how much it will cost you, when it will be open and what to expect. Furthermore, every page has its own map showing the position of each item and the nearest landmark. This allows you to orientate yourself quickly and easily in your new surroundings.
To find what you want to do – having dinner, visiting a museum, going for a walk or shopping for gifts – simply flick through the blue headings and take your pick!

The red section is an alphabetical list of information. It provides essential facts about places and cultural items – 'What are Grotesques & Gargoyles?', 'When is Stratford Mop Fair?', 'Where is Chipping Campden?' – and expands on subjects touched on in the first half of the book. This section also contains practical travel information. It ranges through how to find accommodation, when local events are on, information on music venues, tips on parking, which tours are available and where the youth hostels are. It is lively and informative and easy to use. Each band shows the first three letters of the first entry on the page. Simply flick through the bands till you find the entry you need!

All the main entries are also cross-referenced to help you find them. Names in small capitals – **OXFORD-SHOPPING** – tell you that there is more information about the item you are looking for under the topic on shopping in Oxford in the first part of the book. So when you read 'see **OXFORD-SHOPPING**' you turn to the blue heading for **OXFORD-SHOPPING**. The instruction 'see **A-Z**' after a word, lets you know that the word has its own entry in the second part of the book. Similarly words in bold type – **Falconry** – also let you know that there is an entry in the A-Z for the indicated name. In both cases you just look under the appropriate heading in the red section.
Packed full of information and easy to use – you'll always know where you are with your Collins Traveller Guide!

MAGDALEN GROVE

DEER PARK

Magdalen Bldg

CHRIST CHURCH
MEADOW

Longwall St

Magdalen

St. Edmund
Hall

New
College

University

Merton
Street

Holywell
Street

Queen's Lane

All
Souls

New Coll Ln

Queen's

Oriel

Merton

Catte St

HIGH STREET

Oriel St

Corpus
Christi

Hertford

Exeter

Bear Lane

Brasenose

BROAD STREET

Lincoln

Alfred St

Christ
Church

Ship Street

Jesus

HIGH STREET

Balliol

Market St

St. Aldate's

Magdalen Street

St. Michael's St

GOLDEN
CROSS

CORNMARKET

St. Peter's St

QUEEN ST

THE
COVERED
MARKET

Pembroke Street

Pembroke

Beaumont Street

George Street

New Inn Hall St

ARCADE

St. Ebbe's St

GLOUCESTER
GREEN

Nuffield

New Road

Campion
Hall

Worcester

Worcester St

Hythe Bridge St

Castle Street

ford Canal

Park End Street

Hollybush Row

Oxpens Rd

INTRODUCTION

Around a century ago, novelist Henry James described Stratford and its countryside as 'the core and the centre of the English world; midmost England, unmitigated English'. It is a description that can equally be applied to Oxford and the Cotswolds.* Of course, much has changed since then, and not all for the better. Tourism has largely replaced the role of agriculture and local industries as an employer, villages have depopulated and been re-occupied by city commuters and weekend home-owners, and that modern double-edged sword, the motorcar, has made transport easier but village life increasingly more uncomfortable for those who live there. In many cases, however, tourism has saved Cotswold villages. It was, after all, the Industrial Revolution and not late-20thC 'yuppies' that prompted the original rural exodus and it was upon this scene that William Morris, an ex-Oxford student, entered with considerable implications in the mid-19thC. Morris, one of the leading designers, artists and craftsmen of his time, first 'discovered' the Cotswolds and popularized them in his writings. By a strange coincidence, a few years after his death the British car industry was born at Cowley, near Oxford, thanks to another man named William Morris (no relation). Inevitably, it was the advent of the motorcar that established the Cotswolds as a tourist area in the 1920s and '30s.

It would be interesting to know what William Morris (designer) or William Morris, later Lord Nuffield (car magnate) would make of today's holiday-traffic-congested villages, and particularly the tawdry fast-food stalls at Bourton-on-the-Water. How ironic that the village boasts a splendid motor museum! Fortunately, Bourton-on-a-Bank-Holiday is the exception that proves Henry James' 'rule', as everywhere else you look in this region you cannot help but find charming, old-fashioned England. Cream teas on manicured lawns beside thatched cottages and golden limestone buildings are clichés that come to life with surprising regularity: at Anne Hathaway's Cottage, at Chipping Campden, at Broadway and many other places. Idyllic pubs are also scattered liberally. It's not at all uncommon to find over 300 years of history compressed into a few tiny rooms, and when you've tired of admiring the antique settles, the inglenook fireplace and the ancient pewter you can relax on the riverside terrace, feed the swans and

Anne Hathaway's Cottage

Degree Ceremony at the Sheldonian Theatre, Oxford

watch the gaily painted barges glide by. Even the names of the villages have a triple-barrelled, faintly eccentric English charm. If it's not Chipping this or the other (it means marketplace) it's somewhere or other on-the-Wold, in-Marsh, on-the-Hill, under-Edge, and so on. And imagine the social standing you'll have when you tell your fellow hotel guests you've just spent the day visiting The Barringtons, The Slaughters and The Rissingtons!

For a city holiday, Oxford takes some beating. Unlike many a larger town it is not at all daunting and its compact nature means it can easily be covered on foot. As you would expect from an internationally recognized university centre, the atmosphere is young, lively and cosmopolitan, but as this university is also the oldest in Britain, the sense of history and tradition here is quite unlike anywhere else in Britain, with the possible exception of Cambridge. This unique mix of youth and tradition is captured neatly on film by tourists every year – snapshots of students on bicycles, masters in gowns or senior members in their pink, grey, gold and scarlet robes at the annual Encaenia Procession. You'll sense the University's ancient history most keenly in the tiny college quadrangles (at Merton or St. Edmund Hall, for example) but for real old-world atmosphere visit the cloisters of New College or Magdalen at dusk. The city architecture is also stunning. Quite aside from the colleges and the great Radcliffe Square enclave even the plainest streets and alleyways in the older quarters would be feted elsewhere. Sadly, Arnold's famed 'dreaming spires' no longer dominate the city skyline but the view from the University Church is still a fine sight.

For eating out and shopping, too, Oxford is head and shoulders above the rest of the region, another reflection of its importance as a local centre and the cosmopolitan influences of the University.

Oxford and the Cotswolds also boast some wonderful collections. The Ashmolean Museum is deservedly famous as perhaps Britain's finest provincial museum and gallery, but for many people the most fascinating collection in the city is the Pitt Rivers Museum – 'an extraordinary attic of the human mind' – an ethnographic treasure-trove with over one million pieces. Equally fascinating is the eclectic Charles Wade collection in beautiful Snowshill Manor. The Cotswold Motor Museum at Bourton-on-the-Water is another compelling, atmospheric assemblage which succeeds, like the other places mentioned, in transferring the visitor to a bygone time and distant place.

The region also has an abundance of country houses. All have something to offer but even the most incurious or blasé should find interest in Blenheim Palace and, at the other end of the spectrum in terms of grandeur, the atmospheric Chastleton House. You can see falconry demonstrations and there are some excellent gardens, including Britain's oldest botanic gardens at Oxford and the nationally renowned Hidcote Manor Gardens.

Stratford is much smaller than Oxford and relies almost exclusively on Shakespeare for its tourist dollar but whether or not the Bard moves

you, the five Shakespearean Properties are all worth a visit – and almost incredibly Anne Hathaway's cottage is even prettier than its photographs! There is a fair amount of historical interest in this well-preserved town besides and, of course, if you are remotely interested in the theatre, a night with the Royal Shakespeare Company is a 'must'. Another first-class attraction which far pre-dates Shakespeare lies just north of Stratford: Warwick Castle, claimed to be the finest medieval fortress in England, is everyone's idea of what a castle should be. Sudeley is another fine castle a short car journey from Stratford. There isn't a great deal in the way of participative sport in the region but if you are the outdoor type it does include some of the finest walking countryside in Britain. You'll probably also want to take to the water and, of course, a visit to Oxford wouldn't be complete without taking a punt up the Cherwell.

*For reasons of space, this guide covers only the northern half of the Cotswolds, which are easily accessible from Oxford and Stratford.

Charlecote House

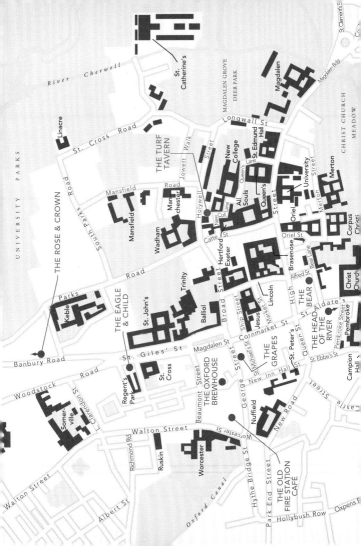

City Pubs

THE BEAR Alfred St.
❑ Traditional hours.
A tiny traditional pub, parts of which date back to the 13thC. Inside is a collection of some 7000 ties and in term time almost as many students!

THE EAGLE & CHILD St. Giles' St.
❑ Traditional hours.
The former haunt of Tolkien and C. S. Lewis, this friendly, old-fashioned pub has several tiny, panelled bars plus a pleasant conservatory area.

THE GRAPES George St.
❑ All-day opening.
Well-preserved Victorian decor with lots of old theatrical prints.

THE HEAD OF THE RIVER St. Aldate's.
❑ All-day opening summer, traditional hours winter.
This former mill house and boat yard enjoys the best riverside position of any Oxford city pub. Popular terrace and balconies overlook the river.

THE OXFORD BREWHOUSE Gloucester St.
❑ Traditional hours.
The split-level interior of this lively pub is quite modern but its bare-brick and stripped-wood finishes combine to give it an antique feel.

THE TURF TAVERN Bath Pl. via St. Helen's Passage.
❑ All-day opening.
An Oxford institution: inside, dark beams, low ceilings and flagstones; outside its three courtyard gardens are very popular. See **OXFORD-WALK 1**.

THE ROSE & CROWN North Parade.
❑ Traditional hours.
This old-fashioned Victorian local retains much of its original charm.

THE OLD FIRE STATION CAFÉ Gloucester Green.
❑ Café bar 1000-1930 Mon.-Sat., 1100-2300 Sun.
Modern arts-centre bar. The decor reflects its former firefighting function.

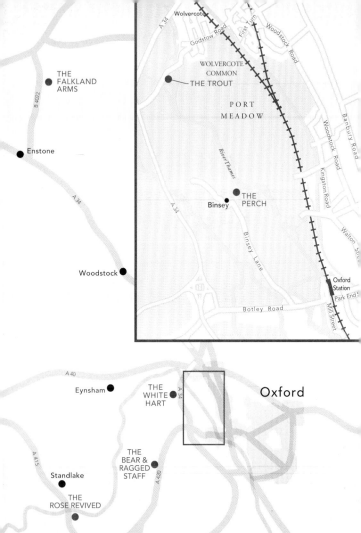

THE
FALKLAND
ARMS

B 4022

Enstone

A 34

Woodstock

Wolvercote

A 34

Godstow Road

Frith Turn

Woodstock Road

WOLVERCOTE
COMMON
THE TROUT

PORT
MEADOW

Woodstock Road

Banbury Road

River Thames

Kingston Road

Binsey

THE
PERCH

Binsey Lane

Walton Stre

Oxford
Station

Park End S

Botley Road

Mill Street

A 40

Eynsham

THE
WHITE
HART

A 34

Oxford

A 415

THE
BEAR &
RAGGED
STAFF

A 420

Standlake

THE
ROSE REVIVED

Country Pubs

THE PERCH Binsey.
❑ Traditional hours Mon.-Fri., all day Sat. 1 mile northwest of Oxford.
Large, thatched pub set in acres of lovely riverside meadows with a huge, open garden. Inside are old-fashioned bare-stone walls, low beams and wooden settles. See **OXFORD-WALK 3***.*

THE TROUT Wolvercote.
❑ All-day opening. 2 miles northwest of the city centre.
An idyllic weir-side setting with terraces and a garden with peacocks make this Oxford's most popular country pub. See **OXFORD-WALK 3***.*

THE WHITE HART Wytham.
❑ Traditional hours. 2.5 miles northwest of the city centre.
Creeper-covered 17thC pub with more of a genuine 'local' feel than The Perch or The Trout, but equally quaint, with a huge inglenook, uneven flagstone floor and tall wooden settles. Great food. See **OXFORD-WALK 3***.*

THE BEAR & RAGGED STAFF Cumnor.
❑ Traditional hours. 4 miles west of Oxford.
Tastefully furnished former 16thC farmhouse with sofas and Turkish-style carpets on its black, mirror-polished flagstones. Good bar food; separate restaurant with a wide and imaginative menu. See **OXFORD-EXCURSION 2***.*

THE ROSE REVIVED Newbridge, near Standlake.
❑ All-day opening summer, traditional hours winter.
9 miles southwest of Oxford.
An idyllic riverside pub (est. 1700) overlooking an ancient bridge and moored rivercraft. Inside is equally delightful, with polished flagstones, antique furnishings, and so on. Reasonably priced bar food. Also has an attractive restaurant. Live jazz on Sun. nights. See **OXFORD-EXCURSION 2***.*

THE FALKLAND ARMS Great Tew.
❑ Traditional hours. 17 miles northwest of Oxford.
A perfect example of a 15thC Cotswold inn, this is one of the great pubs of England, with stone-mullioned windows with wooden shutters, a classic inglenook, wooden settles, and pewter mugs hanging from its beams.

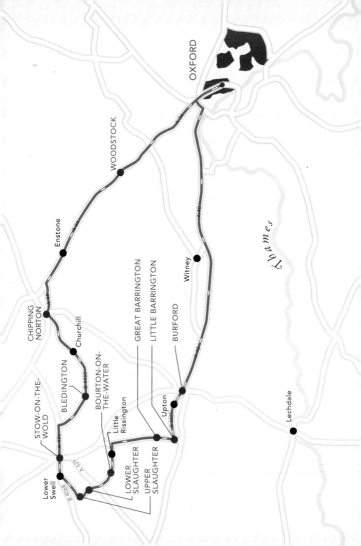

OXFORD

WOODSTOCK

Enstone

CHIPPING
NORTON

Churchill

BLEDINGTON

STOW-ON-THE-
WOLD

Lower Swell

BOURTON-ON-
THE-WATER

Little Rissington

LOWER SLAUGHTER

UPPER SLAUGHTER

GREAT BARRINGTON

LITTLE BARRINGTON

Upton

BURFORD

Witney

Lechlade

Thames

A 429

B 4068

Excursion 1

*A one-day trip from Oxford to some of the most attractive Cotswold villages (see **Cotswolds**). Note that if you wish to start from Stratford you can join the excursion at Chipping Norton. The best days to go are Mon.-Sat.*

Woodstock

Leave Oxford by Woodstock Rd
(A 4144/A 34).
7 miles - Woodstock (see **A-Z**). The gateway to Blenheim Palace (see **OXFORD-HOUSES & PARKS, A-Z**), this attractive market town has an interesting mixture of shops, pubs and restaurants for both tourists and locals. Pass through Enstone and turn left onto the A 44.
19 miles - Chipping Norton. Although this lively market town lies at a busy crossroads it is comparatively untouched by tourism and makes a good coffee stop. Take Banbury Rd (A 361) for a short distance, then turn left onto the B 4450. Pass through Churchill and the pleasant village of Bledington. The King's Head on the green serves good bar food. Just before Stow the B 4450 runs into the A 436.
27 miles - Stow-on-the-Wold (see **A-Z**). This handsome market town lies at the heart of the northern Cotswolds and is famous for its large market square. Leave by the B 4068 (which is a continuation of the A 436) and after one mile you will come to the pretty village of Lower Swell (Swell comes from Our Lady's Well, so it is believed). Turn left, then fork right.
30 miles - Upper Slaughter. Thankfully, the name of this delightful village has nothing to do with bloodshed – it is a derivation of *slohtre*, an Anglo-Saxon term meaning 'muddy place', and as you walk around it and cross the tiny bridge over the River Eye, you can well imagine why. Carry on through the village and turn left.

31 miles - Lower Slaughter. As the hedgerows finish, the 17thC flour mill and its water wheel appear on your left. Behind the mill is the village shop, the only nod to tourism in this immaculate place. The shallow, crystal-clear brook which runs through its centre places it very high in the picture-postcard league. Continue on, turn right onto the A 429 and turn left past The Coach & Horses pub.

33 miles - Bourton-on-the-Water (see **A-Z**). The car park is on the right. This is the most visited and most commercialized village in the Cotswolds. Don't miss Birdland or the Motor Museum. Leave the village on Rissington Rd (past Birdland) and pass through Little Rissington. Fork right, then turn right towards The Barringtons. The disused airfield to your left has RAF and USAF

connections and was formerly the home of the Red Arrows, the RAF stunt-flying team.

39 miles - The Barringtons. 'Great' is separated from 'Little' by a bridge over the Windrush, where The Fox Inn enjoys a picturesque setting. Little Barrington lies around an unusual, deep, saucer-shaped green which was once a quarry. Turn left and follow the B 4425 through Upton to Burford.

42 miles - Burford (see **A-Z**). The High St view of this beautiful large village is a highlight of any Cotswold tour. In particular you should pay a visit to The Lamb, the oldest and finest of Burford's many inns. This 15thC pub is beautifully decorated, with chintzy upholstered settles, flowers on polished antique tables, and so on. There is also a lovely terraced garden.

Return to Oxford on the A 40 (18 miles). Total round trip 60 miles.

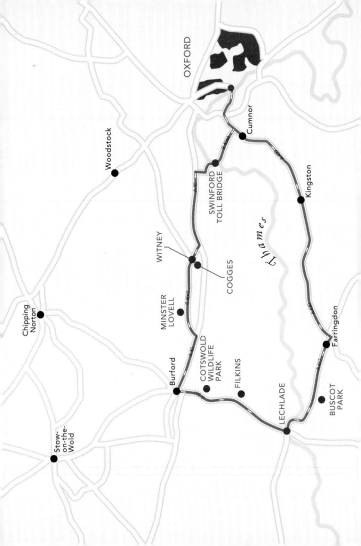

OXFORD

Woodstock

Cumnor

Kingston

SWINFORD
TOLL BRIDGE

Thames

WITNEY

COGGES

MINSTER
LOVELL

Chipping
Norton

Farringdon

Burford

COTSWOLD
WILDLIFE
PARK

FILKINS

LECHLADE

BUSCOT
PARK

Stow-
on-the-
Wold

Excursion 2

*A one-day excursion from Oxford exploring the best of West
Oxfordshire. You may not have time to visit all the places listed below
so try to make your selection before you set out. The best days to go are
Mon.-Sat.*

Leave town by Botley Rd (A 420) past the railway station and carry
straight on as it runs into the B 4044.

5 miles - Swinford Toll Bridge. This 18thC toll bridge is one of only two
left over the Thames and at 2p is very good value! Turn left to join the
busy A 40. After five miles turn right onto the B 4022 towards Witney,
then left to Cogges.

12.5 miles - Cogges Manor Farm Museum. Incongruously set amid a
new housing estate is the ancient hamlet of Cogges. The centrepiece is
the working farm museum (see **OXFORD-HOUSES & PARKS**). See also the
adjacent 14thC church. Backtrack to the B 4022 and turn left.

14 miles - Witney (see **A-Z**). This busy, thriving market town, famous
for the manufacture of blankets, is a good place for shopping and
refreshments. Leave by going down High St, then turn left up Mill Lane
and go past the chimney of Earley Mill onto the B 4047 Burford Rd.
After two miles turn right towards Old Minster.

17 miles - Minster Lovell. Descend into the valley and cross the meadows (an ideal picnic spot) by the ancient, narrow bridge which was
once used as a tally point for sheep en route to London. Ahead and to
the right is The Old Swan, a charming, rough-stone, half-timbered
building which claims to have been a hostelry for 600 years. Continue
up the pretty lane a short distance to St. Kenelm's church and the ruins
of Minster Lovell Hall. The remains of this 15thC manor house are in a
beautiful, peaceful, riverside setting, surrounded by untouched countryside (1000-1800 summer, 1000-1600 Tue.-Sat., winter. 85p, concessions 65p, child 40p). Backtrack and turn right onto the B 4047. Turn
right again onto the A 40 towards Burford and after 2.5 miles turn left
onto the A 361.

22.5 miles - Cotswold Wildlife Park. A fine zoo park where African
animals roam a typically English country scene (1000-1800 or dusk.
£3.20, senior citizen or child £1.90). Turn back, right, onto the A 361
and after two miles turn off to the left.

25 miles - Filkins. This unspoilt village is home to the Cotswold Woollen Weavers, in a fascinating, small weaving mill where you can see the looms worked with old-fashioned punched-card techniques (1000-1800 Mon.-Sat., 1400-1800 Sun. Free). Informative panels tell you the history of the Cotswold wool trade (see **Wool**) and there is a pleasant tearoom and an excellent shop. Continue through Filkins and turn right, back onto the A 361.

29 miles - Lechlade. This pleasant, small, market town lies at the confluence of three rivers, and boats may be hired from here. There are also two riverside pubs on St. John's St (to the left by the church) and Thames St (further on into the town). Visit the lovely 500-year-old church of St. Lawrence and its grassy, atmospheric graveyard which in 1815 inspired Shelley so much that he wrote about it. Leave by St. John's St (A 417), go through Buscot and a mile on the left lies Buscot Park.

32 miles - Buscot Park. An 18thC Adam-style house set in a 55-acre park (see **OXFORD-HOUSES & PARKS**). Continue through Faringdon and turn left onto the A 420. Pass through the villages of Kingston and Cumnor, visiting The Bear & Ragged Staff on Appleton Rd if it is open (see **OXFORD-COUNTRY PUBS**). Note that The Rose Revived (see **OXFORD-COUNTRY PUBS**) and Abingdon (see **A-Z**) are both nearby, making short detours worthwhile if you have time.

Turn left onto the A 34 to return to Oxford (18 miles). Total round trip 50 miles.

WATERPERRY
GARDENS

A 418

A 40

Oxford

A 4095

Thames

BLENHEIM
PALACE

A 4095

A 40

STANTON
HARCOURT
MANOR

A 415

A 420

COGGES
MANOR FARM
MUSEUM

Thames

A 4095

A 40

A 417

A 420

BUSCOT
PARK

Houses & Parks

BLENHEIM PALACE 8 miles north of Oxford.
❏ Palace 1030-1730 (last admission 1645) mid-Mar.-31 Oct.; park and gardens 0900-1700. ❏ All-inclusive ticket £5.40, senior citizen, 16/17-year-old £4.10, child 5-15 £2.65. Park and gardens only £2.75 by car, on foot 70p, child 30p.
One of England's great houses set amid splendid landscaped gardens, Blenheim is world-famous as the birthplace of British wartime prime minister Sir Winston Churchill. See **A-Z***.*

BUSCOT PARK (THE FARINGDON TRUST COLLECTION)
18 miles west of Oxford.
❏ 1400-1800 Wed.-Fri., 2nd, 4th Sat., Sun. in the month.
❏ House and gardens £3, child £1.50. Gardens only £2, child £1.
The plain façade of Buscot House (c.1780) belies its splendid collection of furniture, ceramics, sculptures, old masters and Pre-Raphaelite works, notably Burne-Jones' fine Sleeping Beauty *set. See* **OXFORD-EXCURSION 2***.*

COGGES MANOR FARM MUSEUM 12 miles west of Oxford.
❏ 1030-1730 Tue.-Fri. & hol., 1200-1730 Sat., Sun. ❏ £1.80, child 90p.
This working farm and museum is set around a restored 13th-17thC manor house. The farmyard buildings house many rare breeds. See **OXFORD-EXCURSION 2**, **Wool***.*

STANTON HARCOURT MANOR 9 miles west of Oxford.
❏ 1400-1800 Thu., Sun. (fortnightly only) & hol. (Easter-late Sep.).
❏ House and gardens £3, child under 13 £1.50. Gardens only £1.50, child 75p.
The picturesque manor house and its lovely gardens, both formal and wild, lie in a walled estate overlooking virgin countryside.

WATERPERRY GARDENS 8 miles east of Oxford.
❏ 1000-1730 Mon.-Fri., 1000-1800 Sat., Sun. (1 April-30 Sep.); 1000-1630 1 Oct.-31 Mar. ❏ £1.50, senior citizen £1.10, child 10-16 75p.
Waterperry is informal and relatively compact, with lovely flower borders around large lawns, and alpine and herbaceous nurseries. A river walk, an ancient village church and a fine teashop can also be enjoyed.

St. Clement's St

Cowley

River Cherwell

St. Catherine's

MAGDALEN GROVE
DEER PARK

THE BLUE COYOTE

Magdalen

Magdalen Bdg

CHRIST CHURCH MEADOW

Longwall St

Linacre

St. Cross Road

Jowett Walk

New College

St. Edmund Hall

Queen's Lane

University

Merton

UNIVERSITY PARKS

Mansfield

Road

Man chester

Holywell Street

New College Lane

All Souls

New College Lane

Queen's

High Street

Oriel

Merton Street

Corpus Christi

LUNA CAPRESE

CHERWELL BOATHOUSE

Mansfield

Wadham

Catte St

Hertford

Exeter

Oriel St

Brasenose

Bear Lane

Christ Church

South Parks

Road

Parks

Keble

Trinity

Broad Street

Lincoln

Alfred St

High

St. Aldate's

Banbury Road

St. John's

Balliol

Ship Street

Jesus

Market St

Cornmarket St

St. Peter's

Queen St

LA SORBONNE

Pembroke Street

Pembroke

Woodstock

Road

Regent's Park

St. Cross

Magdalen St

George Street

New Inn Hall St

St. Michael's St

St. Ebbe's St

Campion Hall

THE CRYPT

Castle Street

BROWN'S

Somer ville

L. Clarendon St

Beaumont Street

Nuffield

New Road

Walton Street

Richmond Rd

Ruskin

Worcester St

Worcester

Hythe Bridge St

MUNCHY MUNCHY

Park End Street

Hollybush Row

Oxpens Rd

Walton Street

Albert St

Oxford Canal

Restaurants

LA SORBONNE 130a High St (down the alley), tel: 0865-241320.
❑ 1200-1430, 1900-2300 Tue.-Sat. ❑ Expensive.
This renowned, family-run restaurant, set in a beautiful 17thC house, has been serving the best classic French cuisine in town since 1966.

BROWN'S Woodstock Rd.
❑ 1100-2300 Mon.-Sat., 1200-2330 Sun. & hol. ❑ Moderate.
Oxford's trendiest eating place, where the top-quality English and international dishes and bistro food are worth queuing for (no reservations).

MUNCHY MUNCHY Park End St, tel: 0865-245710.
❑ 1200-1400, 1730-2200 Tue.-Sat. ❑ Moderate (unlicensed; corkage 50p per person).
Spartan decor but excellent Indonesian-Malaysian dishes served at almost fast-food speed from a bustling, open kitchen.

THE BLUE COYOTE St. Clement's St.
❑ 1200-2400 Mon.-Fri., 1000-0200 Sat.-Sun. ❑ Moderate.
American and Mexican food dominate a varied menu but the standard of cooking and friendly service is much higher than an average 'Tex-Mex'.

CHERWELL BOATHOUSE Bardwell Rd, tel: 0865-52746.
❑ 1200-1400, 1830-2130/2200 Tue.-Sat., 1200-1400 Sun.
❑ Moderate.
Converted boathouse offering varied selection of English-inspired dishes.

LUNA CAPRESE North Parade, tel: 0865-54812.
❑ 1200-1430, 1800-2330. ❑ Moderate.
Long-established, lively Italian restaurant hustles and bustles its way through an extensive, interesting menu. Friendly service.

THE CRYPT Frewin Court, off Cornmarket, tel: 0865-251000.
❑ 1130-1500, 1730-2300 Mon.-Fri., 1130-1500, 1800-2300 Sat.
❑ Inexpensive.
Labyrinthine, old English-cellar vaults with a real Dickensian atmosphere. The pies are the pick of a traditional English wine-bar menu.

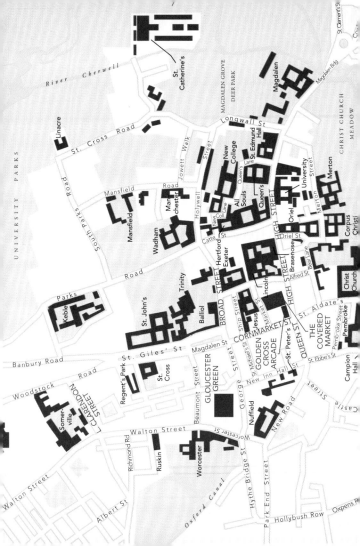

Shopping

BROAD ST

The place for books – old, new, second-hand and rare. Dillons and Blackwells are the best general shops. The old-fashioned Thornton's Booksellers & Buyers (est. 1835) is worth a look. See OXFORD-WALK 2.

CORNMARKET ST/QUEEN ST

These two, unsightly, modern, 'High St' developments comprise a wide cross section of British retailing, including Marks & Spencer, Laura Ashley, Selfridges, Crabtree & Evelyn and Debenhams (Magdalen St).

THE COVERED MARKET

A vibrant, old-fashioned cornucopia of butchers, bakers, poultry and game merchants, fishmongers, fruit-and-vegetable sellers and florists make this place off High St a delight for the senses. See OXFORD-WALK 2.

GLOUCESTER GREEN

A cattle market until 1931, this open square now houses 14 stylish shops and several cafés and restaurants. Rowan (fine wools, designer knitwear, jewellery and gifts) and Once a Tree (top-quality carved wooden items) are particularly notable. Look out for the street performers on Sat.

GOLDEN CROSS ARCADE

This small arcade off Cornmarket St is set around a medieval courtyard and features several higher-class shops, from S'il Vous Plait Belgian Chocolates to Neal's Yard Wholefood & Remedies and several designer-fashion outlets. See OXFORD-WALK 2.

HIGH ST

'The High' features antiques, rare books, gents' and college outfitters and famous names like Liberty and Laura Ashley. If you like preserves head for Frank Cooper's fine shop and small museum, while art lovers will enjoy the Oxford Gallery. Finally, don't miss Past Times in Turl St.

LITTLE CLARENDON ST

The main attraction here is Tumi, a fascinating Latin American crafts shop and gallery featuring pottery, jewellery, music and painted gourds.

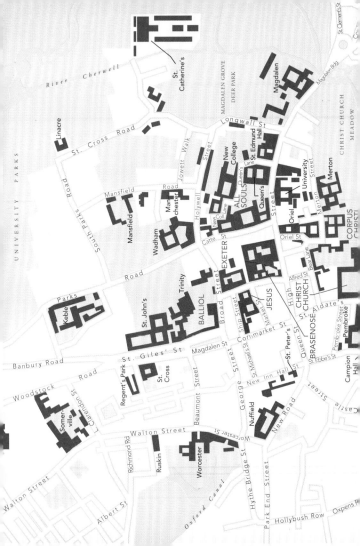

St. Catherine's

Magdalen

St. Cross Road

River Cherwell

MAGDALEN GROVE
DEER PARK

Longwall St

Linacre

Magdalen Bdg

CHRIST CHURCH MEADOW

CHRIST CHURCH

UNIVERSITY PARKS

South Parks Road

Jowett Walk

Mansfield Road

New College

St. Edmund Hall

Mansfield

Manchester

Holywell

New Coll Lane

Queen's Lane

ALL SOULS

Queen's

University

Merton

Wadham

Catte St

Street

Oriel

Merton Street

Oriel St

CORPUS CHRISTI

Parks Road

Keble

Trinity

Broad Street

EXETER

Turl Street

Ship Street

Market St

JESUS

High Street

Alfred St

Bear Lane

CHRIST CHURCH

BRASENOSE

Aldate's

St. John's

BALLIOL

St. Giles' St

Cornmarket St

Magdalen St

St. Peter's

St. Michael's St

Queen St

St. Aldate's

Pembroke Street

Pembroke

St. Ebbe's St

Banbury Road

Parks

Regent's Park

St. Cross

Beaumont Street

George Street

New Inn Hall St

New Road

Campion Hall

Castle Street

Woodstock Road

L. Clarendon St

Somerville

Nuffield

Walton Street

Richmond Rd

Ruskin

Worcester St

Worcester

Hythe Bridge St

Park End Street

Hollybush Row

Oxpens R

Albert St

Oxford Canal

ALL SOULS COLLEGE High St/Radcliffe Sq.
❏ Grounds and chapel 1400-1700.
*The fine frontage and front quad. are 15thC. The inner quad., dominated
by the Hawksmoor towers and sundial, is early-18thC. See* **A-Z**.

BALLIOL COLLEGE Broad St.
❏ Grounds only 1000/1030-1800 or dusk.
*Founded c.1250 but mostly rebuilt during the 19thC. Note the gargoyles
around the library windows in the front quad. See* **OXFORD-WALK 2**.

BRASENOSE COLLEGE Radcliffe Sq.
❏ Grounds and chapel 1000-1700, hall 1000-1200, 1400-1700.
*The Old Quad. dates from the early 16th-17thC. Note the hall's huge
brazen (brass) knocker, origin of the college name. See* **OXFORD-WALK 1**.

CHRIST CHURCH COLLEGE St. Aldate's.
❏ Grounds, cathedral and hall 0930-1800 Mon.-Sat., 0930-1630 Sun.
(summer); 0930-1630 Mon.-Sat., 1400-1730 Sun. (winter). Hall closes
1200-1400, cathedral closes 1645 Mon.-Sat. ❏ £1. ❏ Picture gallery
1030-1300, 1400-1730 Mon.-Sat., 1400-1730 Sun. ❏ 50p.
Oxford's greatest college. Its chapel serves as Oxford's cathedral. See **A-Z**.

CORPUS CHRISTI COLLEGE Merton St.
❏ Grounds and chapel 1330-1730.
*The gateway, front quad. and splendid pelican sundial all date from the
16thC, as does the chapel with its altarpiece from the school of Rubens.*

EXETER COLLEGE Turl St.
❏ Grounds and chapel 1400-1700.
*The Turl St front and quad. are 17th-18thC, though much altered. The
chapel tapestry is by former members William Morris and Burne-Jones.*

JESUS COLLEGE Turl St.
❏ Grounds, chapel and hall 1400-1630.
*Jesus includes two picturesque 17thC quads and a fine hall. Portraits
include Charles I (by Van Dyck) and former member T. E. Lawrence.*

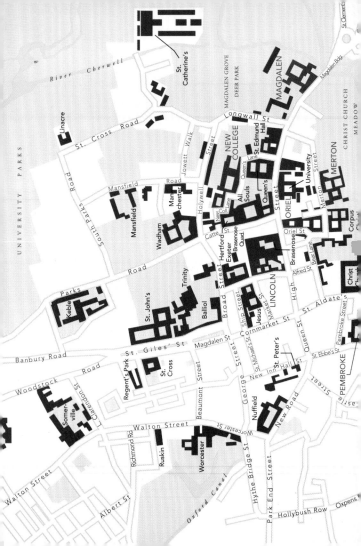

LINCOLN COLLEGE Turl St.

❏ Grounds 1400-1700 Mon.-Sat., 1100-1700 Sun. Chapel, hall, Wesley Room (key at the lodge) and library (Tue., Thu. only) 1430-1630.
The front quad. and timber hall are perfect 15thC survivors. The hall retains its central smoke louvre, and portraits of members include John Wesley. Its beautiful chapel survives in its original state.

MAGDALEN COLLEGE High St.

❏ Grounds and antechapel 1400-1815. ❏ Summer vacation & hol. 75p, child 30p, free rest of the year. Tours during summer vacation & hol., including hall and chapel £1.75, child £1.30.
Oxford's second-largest college has many interesting features. See **A-Z**.

MERTON COLLEGE Merton St.

❏ Grounds 1400-1700 Mon.-Fri., 1000-1700 Sat., Sun. Old Library 1400-1600 Mon.-Sat. (ask at the gatehouse), chapel 1400-1630. College closes 1600 Oct.-Mar.
Most of Merton dates from the 15th-17thC, but the charming 14thC Mob Quad. is the oldest quad. in Oxford. See **A-Z**.

NEW COLLEGE New College Lane.

❏ Grounds, chapel and hall 1400-1700. ❏ 50p out of term-time.
Founded in 1379, New College is one of the city's greatest architectural triumphs. See **OXFORD-WALK 1**, **Grotesques & Gargoyles**, **A-Z**.

ORIEL COLLEGE Oriel Sq.

❏ Grounds 1400-1700.
The picturesque 17thC front quad. is dominated by the statues of two kings, thought to be Edward II and either James VI and I, or Charles I. See **OXFORD-WALK 1**.

PEMBROKE COLLEGE Pembroke St.

❏ Grounds and chapel (key at the gatehouse) 1000-1600.
The inner Chapel Quad. features a fine hall, and the creeper-covered range was once 16thC almshouses. Don't miss the 18thC chapel and look for the plaque to James Smithson (of the Smithsonian Institute).

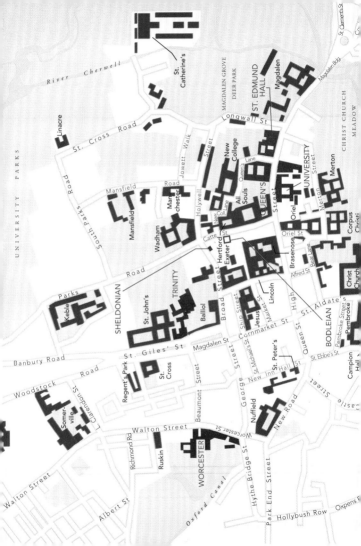

QUEEN'S COLLEGE High St.
❏ Grounds, chapel and hall 1400-1700.
The 18thC classical front quad. is quite unlike most Oxford colleges.
Note the attractive 17thC chapel ceiling painting. See **OXFORD-WALK 1**.

ST. EDMUND HALL Queen's Lane.
❏ Grounds and Norman church crypt (key at the gatehouse) dawn-dusk.
'Teddy Hall' is the last survivor of the medieval student halls and its front
quad. is one of the most charming in the city. See **OXFORD-WALK 1**.

TRINITY COLLEGE Broad St.
❏ Grounds 1400-1700, chapel and hall 1400-1500.
The charming front cottages, gate tower and chapel all date from the
17thC. Fine members' portraits in the hall; beautiful, large grounds.

UNIVERSITY COLLEGE High St.
❏ Admission to the grounds and Shelley Memorial by request.
Queen Anne presides over the fine gate tower while inside is a lovely
17thC quad. See the pompous Shelley Memorial. See **OXFORD-WALK 1**.

WORCESTER COLLEGE Worcester St/Beaumont St.
❏ Grounds and chapel 0900-1200, 1400-1800.
The front quad. comprises 13th and 14thC former monastic houses, and
an 18thC classical range. The grounds are some of the city's finest.

BODLEIAN LIBRARY Radcliffe Sq.
❏ Divinity School free. Tours of Duke Humfrey's Library, Divinity
School and Convocation House 1030, 1130, 1400, 1500 Mon.-Fri.
1030, 1130 Sat. (summer). Reduced winter schedule. ❏ £2.
See the Divinity School (1427-83), one of Oxford's best medieval build-
ings, and the Duke's Library, oldest in Oxford. See **OXFORD-WALK 1, A-Z**.

SHELDONIAN THEATRE Broad St.
❏ 1000-1245, 1400-1645 Mon.-Sat. (mid-Feb. to mid-Nov.). 1000-
1245, 1400-1545 Mon.-Sat. (mid-Nov. to mid-Feb.). ❏ 30p.
A small rotunda theatre, one of Wren's first works. See **OXFORD-WALK 1**.

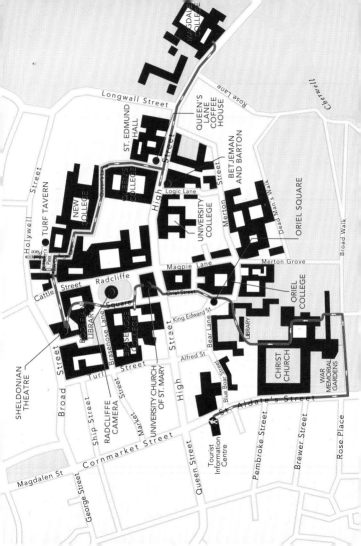

MAGDALEN COLLEGE

Longwall Street

Rose Lane

Cherwell

QUEEN'S LANE COFFEE HOUSE

ST. EDMUND HALL

BETJEMAN AND BARTON

Merton Street

ORIEL SQUARE

Queen's Lane

NEW COLLEGE

QUEEN'S COLLEGE

Holywell Street

Lane

TURF TAVERN

High Street

Logic Lane

UNIVERSITY COLLEGE

Merton Street

Dead Man's Walk

Broad Walk

Cattle Street

Radcliffe Square

Magpie Lane

Merton Grove

ORIEL COLLEGE

BODLEIAN LIBRARY

Brasenose Lane

Oriel Street

LIBRARY

BRASENOSE COLLEGE

High Street

King Edward St.

Bear Lane

SHELDONIAN THEATRE

Broad Street

Turl Street

RADCLIFFE CAMERA

Market Street

UNIVERSITY CHURCH OF ST. MARY

Alfred St.

Blue Boar Street

CHRIST CHURCH

WAR MEMORIAL GARDENS

Ship Street

St. Aldate's Street

George Street

Cornmarket Street

Queen Street

Tourist Information Centre

Pembroke Street

Brewer Street

Rose Place

Magdalen St.

A full day's walking tour into the heart of the city, including visits to at least six of Oxford's most interesting colleges. All the colleges mentioned below, except Hertford, are detailed in **OXFORD-UNIVERSITY 1, 2, 3.**

Start at the Tourist Information Centre on St. Aldate's. Walk down St. Aldate's past the looming Tom Tower of Christ Church and enter the college through the War Memorial Garden. See the hall, the cathedral and the picture gallery (see **Christ Church College, Oxford**). Exit left from the gate by the picture gallery and you are in charming Oriel Square, named after the college on the right-hand side. Look in through the gate to see the fine 17thC porch carved in honour of Charles I and if the college is open, see its grounds. Take the right-hand fork, up Oriel Street. As you appear onto 'the High' (High Street), stop to admire the splendid, twisted columns and 17thC portico of the University Church of St. Mary the Virgin (see **OXFORD-WHAT TO SEE 2**). Cross High Street using the pedestrian crossing, walk through the church and turn left to Brasenose College. Visit the college grounds and the lovely 17thC chapel, then leave by the same gate. The large, round building in the centre of the square is the Radcliffe Camera, designed by James Gibbs in 1749 to house the scientific library of Dr John Radcliffe (camera means 'chamber' or 'room'). It was taken over by the Bodleian Library in 1860 and is now a reading room but unfortunately is not open to the public. To your left is the entrance to the Bodleian Library (see **OXFORD-UNIVERSITY 3, A-Z**). Enter the Schools Quad. of the Bodleian facing the statue of the Earl of Pembroke (Chancellor of the University 1617-30) and get your ticket to join the highly recommended Library tour from the door on your left. After the tour, turn left out of the Schools Quad. and on your left is Sir Christopher Wren's domed Sheldonian Theatre (1663-69; see **OXFORD-UNIVERSITY 3**). The recently restored 13 'Emperors' Heads' around the theatre (which are not really Emperors, but classical Roman and Greek figures) were part of Wren's original design.

You can climb to the top of the cupola for a view over the city's famed 'dreaming spires'. Leaving the Sheldonian, walk straight ahead beneath the Bridge of Sighs, built in 1913-14 as a walkway between the two buildings of Hertford College. A left turn will bring you into the narrow St. Helen's Passage: follow it to The Turf Tavern (see **OXFORD-CITY PUBS**), secluded in a cobbled time warp behind the high walls of Bath Place. Explore beyond The Turf to Holywell Street before coming back to New College Lane. A few yards away on the left is the house where the astronomer Edmund Halley, who first predicted the return to Earth of the famous Comet, lived and had his observatory. The entrance of New College (see **A-Z**), one of the city's oldest and finest architectural group-ings, lies at the end of this lane, and you should take some time to have a look around. Leaving New College, follow the lane to your left,

noting as you go the splendid grotesques and gargoyles (see **A-Z**). The tiny, pretty front quad. of St. Edmund Hall, also a University college, is on your left just before the High. At the High take a tea break at the cheap and cheerful Queen's Lane Coffee House or walk back up the High for about 100 yards and cross the road to the charming tearoom of tea and coffee specialists Betjeman and Barton. Queen's College is immediately to your right and almost opposite Queen's is University College. However, if you only have the energy to see one more college, walk a little further down the High to Magdalen (see **A-Z**). Its elegant buildings and beautiful grounds make for a fitting conclusion to your walk and you can finish the day by attending Evensong to hear the famous choir.

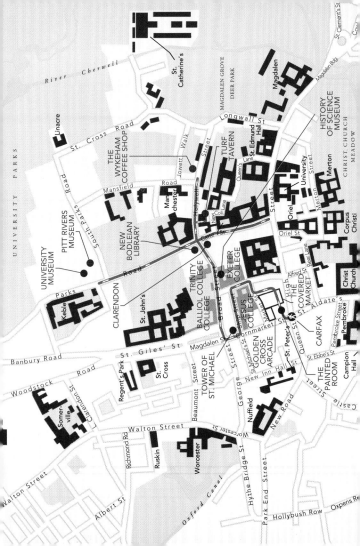

A busy half-day or a leisurely full-day walk around some of Oxford's oldest non-University buildings, taking in some fine shops. The best days to go are Mon.-Fri. so you can see The Painted Room.

Start at Carfax facing down High Street. This 14thC tower is all that remains of the old church of St. Martin. Turn left into Cornmarket Street and a few yards on the right (just before the Golden Cross Arcade) is the entrance to number 3. Although there is no sign to tell you it is there, behind the ugly, modern facade lies The Painted Room (see **OXFORD-WHAT TO SEE 2**), a part of the 16thC Crown Tavern. William Shakespeare (see **A-Z**) is thought to have used this hostelry frequently en route from London to Stratford and tradition has it that the Bard may have cuckolded the landlord, John Davenant, here in the Painted Room, thus conceiving William Davenant (1606-68), Shakespeare's only son to survive to adulthood. Turn right into the Golden Cross Arcade (see **OXFORD-SHOPPING**) to continue the Shakespeare connection. The 13thC courtyard here was probably the stage for some of the Bard's plays (spectators would have been drinking in the old Golden Cross Inn) and here also England's best-known Reformation martyrs, Archbishop Thomas Cranmer and Bishops Hugh Latimer and Nicholas Ridley were jailed. Explore the excellent Victorian Covered Market (see **OXFORD-SHOPPING**) and exit right into Market Street. Follow this round to your left, into Turl Street, and almost opposite each other are the gatehouses to Exeter College (see **OXFORD-UNIVERSITY 1**) and Jesus College (see **OXFORD-UNIVERSITY 1**). Turn left into Ship Street. The ancient building on the corner with Cornmarket Street (now home to a branch of Laura Ashley) is thought to have been built in 1389 as the New Inn. On the other side of Ship Street is Oxford's oldest structure, the Saxon Tower of St. Michael, standing on the former site of the city wall's north gate (see **OXFORD-WHAT TO SEE 2**). Turn right into Broad Street, long renowned as Oxford's 'best-read' street (see **OXFORD-SHOPPING**). Almost opposite The Oxford Story (see **OXFORD-WHAT TO SEE 1**) and set in the middle of the road is a stone cross to commemorate the spot where Cranmer, Latimer and Ridley were burned at the stake by Mary I ('Bloody Mary') in 1555 and 1556. The gates of Balliol College (see **OXFORD-UNIVERSITY 1**) opposite were scorched by the flames and

you can still see these, now repositioned, between the front quad. and inner quad., although the marks may be hidden if the doors are locked open against the wall. Further along Broad Street is Trinity College (see **OXFORD-UNIVERSITY 3**) and opposite is the 17thC Old Ashmolean Museum building, now home to the Museum of the History of Science (see **OXFORD-WHAT TO SEE 1**). Next door (beyond the rotund Sheldonian Theatre) is the Clarendon Building, built in 1713 for the Oxford University Press (OUP) and, by contrast, opposite that lies the 'brutal-ist'-style 20thC block housing the New Bodleian Library (see **Bodleian Library, Oxford**).

At this point you have several options: to turn left into Parks Road to the excellent collections of the University Museum (see **OXFORD-WHAT TO SEE 2**) and the Pitt Rivers Museum (see **OXFORD-WHAT TO SEE 2**, **A-Z**); to continue straight ahead along Holywell Street and either go to The Wykeham Coffee Shop, a small, homely tearoom with an outdoor patio, or turn right into St. Helen's Passage to The Turf Tavern (see **OXFORD-CITY PUBS**) from where you can pick up **WALK 1**; or to turn right down Catte Street to return to High Street.

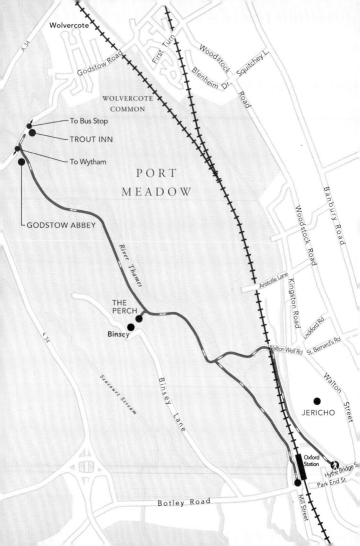

Walk 3

A circular walk out of town across Port Meadow and Binsey fields, taking in three of Oxford's best and nearest country pubs. You can also cycle along this route but take care by the water's edge! The best time to go is when the pubs are open. For details of all the pubs see OXFORD-COUNTRY PUBS.

Descend the steps from Hythe Bridge Street to the Oxford Canal towpath, so-called because horses used the path while towing goods-laden barges along here. The canal was opened in the late 18thC and was used to carry coal and industrial commodities from the north and the Midlands to Oxford and to take back farm produce the other way. The brightly coloured barges you'll see today are used as houseboats and pleasure craft. Across the canal is the 19thC suburb of Jericho and the College Cruisers boatyard. Continue until you come to the Walton Well Road bridge, then walk up the steps, turn left and the road will soon end. Ahead is the beautiful expanse of Port Meadow where you may well see horses roaming as if wild. Walk directly across the Meadow, cross the weir and either turn back (left) to town or continue (right) along the Thames towpath. In Oxford the Thames is also known as the Isis after its ancient name Thamesis. The Perch at Binsey is half a mile from here. Another mile further along the towpath at Wolvercote is The Trout. Just before the pub you will see on your left the ruins of Godstow Abbey. The Trout was originally the 12thC hospice of the Benedictine nunnery at Godstow. As you are supping your drink on the terrace of this lovely pub you may also like to reflect that it was on this stretch of water that Lewis Carroll (Charles L. Dodgson) first told the story of *Alice in Wonderland* to Alice Liddell and two of her young friends while on a boating trip back in 1865 (see **Christ Church College, Oxford**). If you wish to go on to another fine country pub, The White Hart at Wytham, or would simply like to see this lovely village, walk back over the bridge and carry on for less than half a mile. You can catch a bus back to Oxford from Wolvercote (a five-min walk away) or walk back the same way as far as the weir. Cross it and continue back to town along the towpath which will take you in via the railway station.

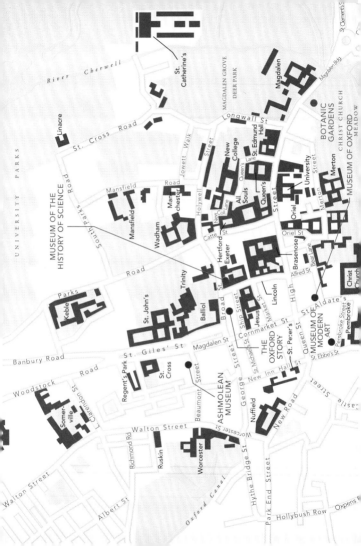

ASHMOLEAN MUSEUM Beaumont St.
❏ 1000-1600 Tue.-Sat., 1400-1600 Sun., 1400-1700 Summer Bank
Hol. Mon. Closed Christmas, Easter and early Sep. (during St. Giles'
Fair). ❏ Free.
*One of Britain's finest provincial museums with an internationally
renowned collection of art and antiquities. See* **A-Z**.

BOTANIC GARDENS High St.
❏ Gardens 0900-1700 during BST, 0930-1630 during GMT (last
admission 15 min before closing). Greenhouses 1400-1600. ❏ Free.
*Britain's oldest botanic gardens, founded in 1621. Superb glasshouses
and formal, woodland and rock gardens form a most serene enclave.*

MUSEUM OF THE HISTORY OF SCIENCE Broad St.
❏ 1030-1300, 1430-1600 Mon.-Fri. Closed Christmas and Easter weeks
and Bank Hol. ❏ Free.
*A collection of early scientific hardware housed in the old Ashmolean
Museum. Clocks, optical, chemical and medical instruments and other
items, often works of art in their own right. See* **OXFORD-WALK 2**.

MUSEUM OF MODERN ART Pembroke St.
❏ 1000-1800 Tue.-Sat., 1400-1800 Sun. ❏ £1, concessions, child 50p.
*A changing programme of innovatively staged modern and contem-
porary exhibitions is held in this skilfully converted 19thC brewery
warehouse. Fine bookshop and excellent café (closes 1700).*

MUSEUM OF OXFORD St. Aldate's.
❏ 1000-1700 Tue.-Sat. ❏ Free.
*An excellent introduction to both 'town and gown' in the city, including
local traditions and customs. The best displays are upstairs and feature a
series of room sections from the 18thC onwards.*

THE OXFORD STORY Broad St.
❏ 0930-1700 April-June, Sep.-Oct.; 0930-1900 July-Aug.; 1000-1600
Nov.-Mar. ❏ £3, child under 16 50p.
A rather uninspiring trip through historical tableaux. See **OXFORD-WALK 2**.

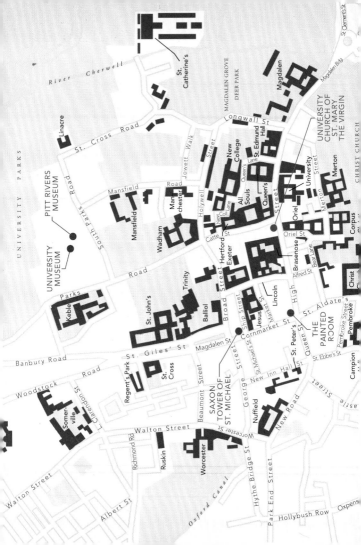

OXFORD

What to See 2

THE PAINTED ROOM 3 Cornmarket St (not marked on the street).
❑ 1000-1700 Mon.-Fri. ❑ Free.
*Now the Oxford Community Church office, this room was formerly part
of the 16thC Crown Tavern and retains original, painted plaster walls
and wood panelling. See* OXFORD-WALK 2.

PITT RIVERS MUSEUM University Museum, Parks Rd.
❑ 1300-1730 Mon.-Sat. ❑ Free.
*One of the world's greatest ethnologic and prehistoric-craft collections,
featuring eye-popping exhibits from all over the tribal world. See*
OXFORD-WALK 2, **Children**, **A-Z**.

SAXON TOWER OF ST. MICHAEL Cornmarket St.
❑ 1000-1700 Mon.-Sat. (April-Oct.), 1000-1600 Mon.-Sat., 1230-1600
Sun. (Nov.-Mar.). ❑ £1, concessions 60p, child 30p.
*This is the easiest of the tower ascents in the city and takes you past a
small treasury and the 17thC church bells and mechanism. The tower of
the 13thC church is Oxford's oldest structure, predating 1050. See*
OXFORD-WALK 2.

UNIVERSITY CHURCH OF ST. MARY THE VIRGIN High St.
❑ Tower 0900-1900 May-Sep., 0930-dusk Oct.-April. ❑ 75p, child
40p. ❑ Brass-rubbing centre 1000-1700 Mon.-Sat., 1200-1700 Sun.
(Sun. opening July, Aug. only).
*The Congregation House of this ancient church (now the coffee shop)
was once the centre of the University administration and the University
Sermon is preached here every Sun. Climb the 13thC tower for the best
view of Oxford. See* OXFORD-WALK 1.

UNIVERSITY MUSEUM Parks Rd.
❑ 1200-1700 Mon.-Sat. ❑ Free.
*The soaring Gothic arches and Crystal Palace-style iron-and-glass roof
are a dramatic setting for the dinosaur skeletons prominent among the
museum's large natural history collection. A dodo and a gemstones collection are other popular exhibits. See* OXFORD-WALK 2, **Children**.

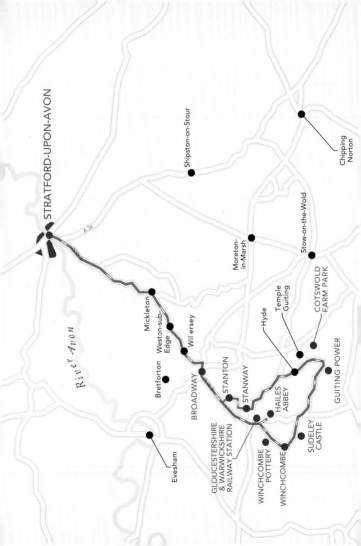

STRATFORD-UPON-AVON

River Avon

Chipping Norton

Shipston-on-Stour

Moreton-in-Marsh

Stow-on-the-Wold

COTSWOLD FARM PARK

Temple Guiting

Hyde

GUITING POWER

Mickleton

Weston-sub-Edge

Wilersey

Bretforton

BROADWAY

STANTON

STANWAY

HAILES ABBEY

SUDELEY CASTLE

Evesham

GLOUCESTERSHIRE & WARWICKSHIRE RAILWAY STATION

WINCHCOMBE POTTERY

WINCHCOMBE

A 34

Excursion 1

*A one-day trip to some outstanding and individual Cotswold villages (see **Cotswolds**), a charming small museum and a historic castle. The best days to go are Tue. or Thu. if you wish to see Stanway House.*

Leave Stratford on the A 34. After one mile turn right onto the B 4632. Pass through Mickleton, Weston-sub-Edge and Willersey.

14 miles - Broadway (see **A-Z**).
The car park is at the entrance to the village. Broadway is a beautiful 'show village' set around the broad High St which is lined with fine 17th and 18thC houses. Turn right onto High St and drive through the village following the B 4632, signposted for Cheltenham. After five miles you will see on your left the restored Gloucestershire & Warwickshire Railway station with vintage trains on display. A steam service runs from here to Winchcombe. One mile further on, turn left.

21 miles - Hailes Abbey. Park by the 12thC parish church and step inside to see its rare medieval wall paintings. The Abbey, an important 13thC pilgrimage centre, lies in ruins but it is a peaceful, secluded spot and has a small museum (1000-1800 summer, 1000-1600 winter. £1.15, concessions 85p, child 60p). Return to the main road and turn left.

23 miles - Winchcombe Pottery. A small, working pottery where you can see craftspeople at work (0800-1200, 1400-1700 Mon.-Fri.).

24 miles - Winchcombe (see **A-Z**). A delightful, uncommercialized village with a very different atmosphere from Broadway. The unusual Railway Museum and Sudeley Castle (see **A-Z**) are 'musts'. After seeing the castle, exit right from the car park (towards Stow-on-the-Wold) and follow the narrow, winding lanes.

30 miles - Guiting Power. Ye Olde Inne makes a good refreshment stop in this pretty village. Continue through the village, then turn either left towards Temple Guiting, or right if you wish to divert to the Cotswold Farm Park, a rare farm-breeds survival centre where you can see old Gloucester cattle, four-horned sheep and Iron Age pigs (1030-1800 Easter-Sep. £2.40, senior citizen £1.75, child £1.20; see **Wool**). Bypass Temple Guiting, go through Hyde and turn left (towards Tewkesbury), making a steep, wooded descent.

38 miles - Stanway. Turn right at the crossroads marked by the monument of St. George and the Dragon and a little way ahead of you looms the striking gatehouse of Stanway House, built between 1580 and 1640 (1400-1700 Tue., Thu., June-Aug. £1.75, senior citizen £1.50, child 75p). One mile further on, turn right.

39 miles - Stanton. A beautiful, unspoilt village with a lovely church. Before turning off, past Stanton's shop, to continue the excursion, drive straight ahead, 200 yards up the hill to the car park of The Mount Inn, for a scenic view.

Continue and turn right, back to Stratford via Broadway (17 miles). Total round trip 56 miles. The Fleece at Bretforton (see **STRATFORD-PUBS**), an outstanding pub even by Cotswold standards, is a rewarding diversion and lies 2.5 miles away after a left turn off the B 4035 from Weston-sub-Edge.

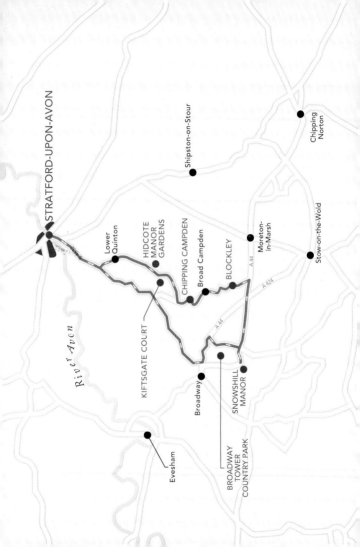

STRATFORD-UPON-AVON

River Avon

Lower Quinton

HIDCOTE MANOR GARDENS

KIFTSGATE COURT

CHIPPING CAMPDEN

Broad Campden

BLOCKLEY

Shipston-on-Stour

Chipping Norton

Moreton-in-Marsh

Stow-on-the-Wold

A 44

A 424

A 44

Broadway

SNOWSHILL MANOR

BROADWAY TOWER COUNTRY PARK

Evesham

A one-day excursion into the beautiful Cotswolds countryside (see **A-Z**), *including a visit to Snowshill Manor. The best days to go are Sat. or Sun.*

Follow **STRATFORD-EXCURSION 1** from Stratford to Broadway (14 miles) and turn left along Broadway's High St (A 44 to Stow).

15 miles - Broadway Tower Country Park. At 1024 ft (335 m) this is the highest point in the north Cotswolds (see **Wool**). It's a great place for families, with walking trails, a children's farmyard and a good tearoom. Climb up the 18thC folly tower for a panoramic view (1000-1800 April-Oct. £1.75, concessions and child £1). Exit right (away from the way you came in) and follow the narrow road for 0.75 mile, turn right and after 0.25 mile turn right again, then right again after 0.5 mile.

17.25 miles - Snowshill Manor (see **A-Z**). In the fine manor house next to the row of picture-postcard cottages you'll find the Cotswolds' most fascinating and unusual collection of objects (1100-1300, 1400-1800 Wed.-Sun. & hol., May-Sep.; 1100-1300, 1400-1700 Sat.-Sun., April, Oct.). Go back up the hill towards Chipping Campden and turn left, then right. After five miles you will cross the busy A 424/A 44. Turn right 100 yards further on, onto the A 44 and then go left to Blockley.

25 miles - Blockley. Park by the church to see its impressive monuments. If you leave the churchyard by the side gate, High St – leading along to The Crown Inn, a good watering-hole – is just around the corner. Turn your car around and continue straight on to Chipping Campden via the pretty village of Broad Campden.

29 miles - Chipping Campden (see **A-Z**). You will enter the town via Sheep St and from there you should turn right onto High St to park. Once you have had a chance to look around this prosperous old town, continue up High St on the B 4035 with the huge church to your right. After 0.25 mile turn right, then fork to the right and turn left at the next crossroads, towards Hidcote Manor Gardens.

33 miles - Kiftsgate Court/Hidcote Manor Gardens. To the left is Kiftsgate, while Hidcote (1100-1900 Mon., Wed., Thu., Sat., Sun., April-Oct. £3.50, child £1.75, family £9.60) is a mile up the road to the right. Both possess outstanding gardens.

Follow the road via Lower Quinton to the B 4632 which leads back to Stratford on the A 34 (9 miles). Total round trip 42 miles.

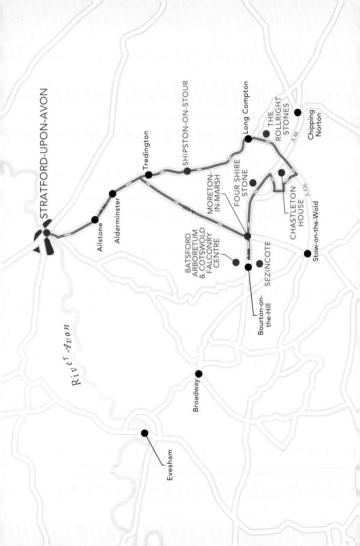

A day's outing for nature and history buffs, visiting an arboretum, a falconry centre, gardens, a house where time seems to have stood still, and some prehistoric monuments. The best day to go is Fri., as this is the only time when all the places featured are open.

Take the A 34 south from Stratford passing through Ailstone and Alderminster. After eight miles turn right onto the A 429 (also known as Fosse Way, as it was originally one of the main Roman roads across Britain).

16 miles - Moreton-in-Marsh. Much of the charm of this crossroads town is spoilt by the thundering traffic but its High St does have some interesting 18th and 19thC buildings. The Market Hall in the centre of town dates from 1887 and the bell of the adjacent tiny 16thC curfew tower was rung each evening to call the labourers home from the fields, until 1860. Turn right onto the A 44 (towards Broadway) and after two miles the entrances to Batsford Arboretum and Sezincote lie opposite each other.

18 miles - Batsford Arboretum & Cotswold Falconry Centre. Climb to the highest point of this lovely 19thC arboretum (1000-1700 April-Nov. £2, senior citizen, child £1). You will be rewarded by a marvellous view over the ivy-covered manor house; then descend to the neo-Norman church. Afterwards you can watch an exciting demonstration of the centuries-old sport of falconry (1030-1730 Mar.-Nov. £2, senior citizen £1.50, child 4-14 £1; flying times 1130, 1330, 1500, 1630, subject to weather; see **Falconry**). For refreshments, try the very pleasant tearooms. This is also the perfect spot for a picnic.

20 miles - Sezincote. Although this house boasts fine landscaped gardens, most people come to admire the famous Indian styling of the house (1805), a striking mixture of Hindu and Moslem with a single large, green, onion dome and four small minarets (gardens 1400-1800 Thu., Fri., Bank Hol. Mon.; closed Dec. House 1430-1800 Thu., Fri. May-July, Sep.). Continue a little way up the hill and a small loop to your left will show you the unspoiled village of Bourton-on-the-Hill. Return to Moreton-in-Marsh and after 1.5 miles on your left is the Four Shire Stone, an 18thC monument marking the boundaries of Gloucestershire, Oxfordshire, Warwickshire and Worcestershire.

One mile further on, turn right.

26 miles - Chastleton House. This atmospheric Stuart house (1603) is quite unlike any other country house in this region, being almost untouched by restoration and with much of its original furniture and decor. Its sad state of repair adds to its ancient atmosphere (1400-1700, last tour 1600 Fri., Sun., Bank Hol. Mon. £2.50, child £1.50).

See also the adjacent medieval church. Continue through the small village, turn right, and then left onto the A 436. Cross the A 44 and bear left.

30 miles - The Rollright Stones. The name of this stone formation, built c.1500 BC for unknown ritual purposes, comes from the nearby village. To the right of the road is 'The King's Men', a 100-ft-wide circle of some 77 boulders, and to the left is the solitary 'King Stone' and a marvellous view. Leaflets on sale here will tell you the legend behind the names. Continue ahead and turn left onto the A 34. Pass through the pleasant village of Long Compton.

37 miles - Shipston-on-Stour. Once an important market centre for sheep (its name probably derives from 'Sheep's Town'; see **Wool**) and then a staging post, Shipston is still a busy town with a pleasant High St and marketplace.

Return to Stratford via the elegant village of Tredington (11 miles). Total round trip 48 miles.

BROUGHTON CASTLE 16 miles southeast of Stratford.

❏ 1400-1700 Wed., Sun. (mid-May to mid-Sep.); Thu. also, July & hol.
❏ £2.30, concessions £1.80, child £1.20.
This fortified manor house (c.1300) has the moat, battlements and curtain wall of a small castle. It was converted to a Tudor mansion c.1550.

CHARLECOTE PARK 5 miles east of Stratford.

❏ House 1100-1300, 1400-1700 Tue., Wed., Fri.-Sun., Bank Hol. Mon.
(April-Oct.). Grounds 1100-1800. ❏ £3, family £8.50.
*Built c.1558 but only its fine gatehouse remains in its original condition.
The grounds and deer park are ideal for a picnic. See **Falconry**, **Tours**.*

KENILWORTH CASTLE 13 miles north of Stratford.

❏ 1000-1800 Mon.-Sat. (April-Sep.), 1000-1600 Tue.-Sun. (Oct.-Mar.).
❏ £1.15, concessions 85p, child 5-16 60p.
*Once of military importance, the castle was destroyed after the Civil War
(1642-48) and is now one of England's largest and most dramatic ruins.*

RAGLEY HALL 8 miles west of Stratford.

❏ House 1200-1700 Tue., Sat. (April-Oct.). Grounds 1000-1800.
❏ Grounds £2.50, child £1.50; grounds & house £3.50, child £2.50.
*Originally built in the 1680s Ragley has been restored to become a
lived-in stately home. Its handsome interiors contrast modern and
antique styles and it features a fine, baroque plasterwork-decorated hall.*

UPTON HOUSE 10 miles southeast of Stratford.

❏ 1400-1800 Sat., Sun. & hol. (April), Sat.-Wed. (May-Sep.), Sat., Sun.
(Oct.). ❏ £2.80, child £1.40, family £7.70; gardens only £1.80.
*Late-17thC house famous for its collection of old masters, including
El Greco, Brueghel, Canaletto and English artists Stubbs and Hogarth.*

WARWICK CASTLE 9 miles northeast of Stratford.

❏ 1000-1800 Mar.-Oct.; 1000-1700 Nov.-Feb. ❏ £4.99, senior citizen
£3.75, child 4-16 £3.25; family £14.50/£16.50 (2/3 children).
*14thC stronghold with huge, fortified keeps and towers, a splendid
armoury, dungeons and magnificent rooms and apartments. See **A-Z**.*

Pubs

ALVESTON MANOR HOTEL Banbury Rd.
⌐ All-day opening.
This Tudor-style hotel was formerly a 16thC manor house and the bar retains some of its original oak panelling. The gardens are famous as the setting for the original production of A Midsummer Night's Dream.

BLACK SWAN Waterside.
⌐ 1030-1600, 1730-2300 Mon.-Sat., traditional hours Sun.
The 'Dirty Duck' is one of the town's most popular pubs, not least for its fine location on a terrace overlooking the riverside gardens. The walls are lined with theatrical faces and you may spot a star in the flesh here.

THE GARRICK INN High St.
⌐ All-day opening.
The splendidly restored front of this building dates back to 1569 and it became a pub in the 18thC, named after the actor David Garrick. Its tiny but quaint rooms have a convivial atmosphere. See **STRATFORD-WALK**.

THE OLD THATCH TAVERN Rother St/Greenhill St.
⌐ All-day opening.
It's no longer thatched but it is old (its license goes back to 1627) and has the character of a basic 'local'. The inside is dark, with heavy beams and stone floors; outside there is a small courtyard with a serving hatch.

WHITE SWAN Rother St.
⌐ All-day opening.
This hotel is thought originally to have been a merchant's home, built c.1450, but it has been a hostelry for over 400 years. The Oak Room, so named for its Jacobean panelling, exudes quiet luxury, with cushioned armchairs, carved settles, attractive fireplaces and a 16thC wall painting.

THE FLEECE Bretforton.
⌐ All-day opening.
One of the most acclaimed pubs in the country, the Fleece is adminis-tered by the National Trust. Features inside include antique settles, Stuart pewter, and casks above the inglenook. See **STRATFORD-EXCURSION 1**.

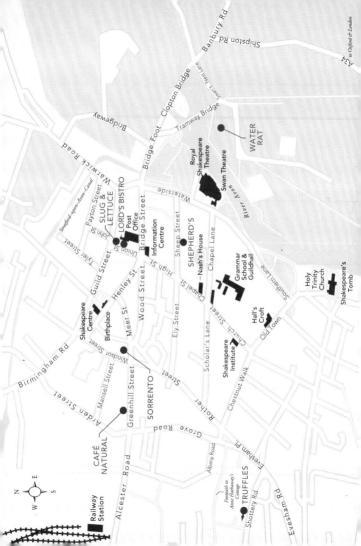

Restaurants

SHEPHERD'S Stratford House Hotel, Sheep St, tel: 0789-68233.
❏ 1200-1400, 1745-1930 (last orders) Tue.-Sat.
❏ Expensive.
Fine English and French country dishes are laid out on pink-and-white starched linen in an elegant conservatory, romantically floodlit by night.

SORRENTO Meer St, tel: 0789-69304.
❏ 1200-1400, 1800-2330 Tue.-Sat., 1800-2330 Mon. Closed mid-Aug.-early Sep. ❏ Moderate-Expensive.
Beautiful setting upstairs in a 16thC black-and-white timbered house, with interesting daily specials and a mouthwatering dessert trolley.

THE SLUG & LETTUCE Guild St/Union St.
❏ 1200-1400, 1800-2200 Mon.-Sat., 1200-1330, 1900-2130 Sun.
❏ Moderate.
This lively pub-cum-bistro is the place to be seen in Stratford. A changing menu features English-inspired dishes with interesting variations.

TRUFFLES Shottery (opposite The Bell Inn), tel: 0789-292039.
❏ 1930-2130 (last orders) Wed.-Sat. ❏ Moderate.
Charming small restaurant with country-cottage atmosphere. The varying menu features a small range of top-quality, English-based dishes.

LORD'S BISTRO Union St, tel: 0789-69106.
❏ 1200-1500, 1730-2300. ❏ Inexpensive-Moderate.
Small, cosy, relaxed bistro with pine panelling and a flagstone floor.

THE WATER RAT CAFÉ BRASSERIE Swan's Nest Lane,
tel: 0789-414658.
❏ 0900-2330 downstairs, 1700-2300 Tue.-Sat. upstairs. ❏ Inexpensive.
Modern, polygonal building with a fine view across the river. Standard brasserie fare downstairs, and upstairs a Spanish tapas bar.

CAFÉ NATURAL Stratford Health Foods, Greenhill St.
❏ 0900-1700 Mon.-Thu., Sat., 0900-1930 Fri. ❏ Inexpensive.
Friendly, unpretentious, wholefood café/restaurant.

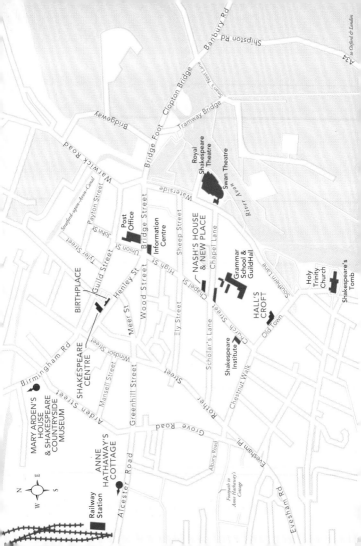

Shakespeare

❏ *Birthplace and Anne Hathaway's Cottage 0900-1800 Mon.-Sat., 1000-
1800 Sun. (summer); 0930-1630 Mon.-Sat., 1030-1630 Sun. (winter).
Other properties 0930-1730 Mon.-Sat., 1030-1730 Sun. (summer);
1000-1630 Mon.-Sat., 1330-1630 Sun. (winter).* ❏ *Joint ticket to all
properties £6, child £2.50. Joint ticket to Birthplace, Hall's Croft and
New Place £4, child £1.80 (buy at Birthplace). See* **A-Z**, **Tours**.

BIRTHPLACE & THE SHAKESPEARE CENTRE Henley St.
❏ Birthplace and costume exhibition £2.20, child 90p.
*The Birthplace comprises two houses – one a typical period home, the
other now a museum. Access is via the modern Shakespeare Centre.*

NEW PLACE/THOMAS NASH'S HOUSE Chapel St.
❏ £1.50, child 60p.
*New Place, to which Shakespeare retired in 1611, was demolished in
1759. Now covered by a colourful garden, it stood beside Nash's House.
Nash was the husband of Shakespeare's granddaughter, Elizabeth Hall.*

HALL'S CROFT Old Town.
❏ £1.50, child 60p.
*Dr John Hall married Shakespeare's daughter, Susanna, in 1607 and they
lived in this splendid late-16thC town house until 1616. It includes fine
furniture, a dispensary and an attractive garden. Afternoon tea available.*

ANNE HATHAWAY'S COTTAGE Shottery, 1.5 miles west of
Stratford. Guide Friday bus; S1 minibus; 20-30 min walk by footpath.
❏ £1.80, child 80p.
*The house dates from c.1463. Anne was born here in 1556 and lived
here for 26 years. Its 12 rooms contain family furniture.*

MARY ARDEN'S HOUSE & SHAKESPEARE COUNTRY-
SIDE MUSEUM Wilmcote, 3.5 miles north of Stratford. Guide
Friday bus; train to Wilmcote. ❏ £2.50, child £1.
*This Tudor farmhouse was the home of Shakespeare's mother in the mid-
16thC and continued to be inhabited up to 1930.*

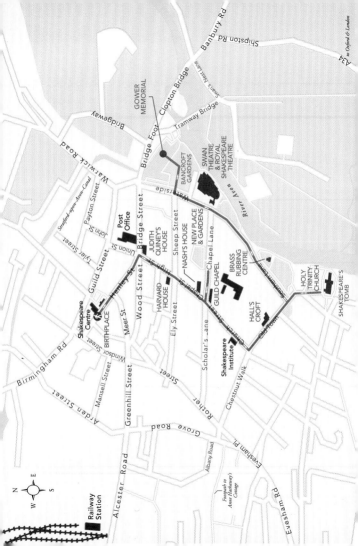

Walk

*A walk in the footsteps of the Bard, from his birthplace to his grave and memorial (see **Shakespeare, William**). Allow a full day if visiting the Shakespearean Properties (see **A-Z**) in town. For details of these, see* **STRATFORD-SHAKESPEARE**.

Start at the Birthplace and see the room where, according to tradition, William Shakespeare was born on 23rd April 1564. Turn left out of the Birthplace and walk down Henley Street to the small roundabout. The 16thC house across the road on the corner of Bridge Street and High Street was the home of Shakespeare's daughter, Judith (Quiney), from 1616-52. It was once used as a lock-up for local wrong-doers and nick-named 'The Cage'. Bear right, along High Street, and on your right is Harvard House, built in 1596. An American link is provided by Katherine Rogers, the daughter of the house builder, Thomas Rogers (look up to see his carved initials). She was the mother of John Harvard who founded the famous university. Harvard House is occasionally open to the public.

Adjacent is The Garrick Inn (see **STRATFORD-PUBS**) and next to that The Old Tudor House, two other properties Shakespeare would have known. Diagonally opposite is The Town Hall, built in 1769. Note the statue of Shakespeare, presented by David Garrick, the greatest English actor of the 18thC, and the faded wording 'God Save the King', refer-ring to King George III. Even the bank opposite (built in 1883) has a Shakespearean theme, with a relief featuring scenes from his plays. Go on up Chapel Street and to your left is The Shakespeare Hotel, formerly the houses of local merchants. This and The Falcon (a little further on) are two of the town's oldest hostelries and both buildings would have been known by the Bard, although in his day neither were inns.

Continue to New Place/Thomas Nash's House, where Shakespeare lived in retirement and died on his 52nd birthday, 23rd April 1616, after some months' illness. Walk up Chapel Lane and enter the tranquil Great Garden of New Place. The ancient, gnarled mulberry tree here is said to have been grown from a cutting which was planted by the Bard. Return to Chapel Street and visit the Guild Chapel (0900-1600). Much of it dates from the late 15thC but the faded wall painting, *The Day of Judgement* or *The Doom* (see the small picture at the back of the

chapel), is much older. The adjacent half-timbered range was built 1416-18 and has been used as the Stratford Grammar School since 1547 (no entry to the public). It is thought that young William attended here, and his desk is exhibited in the Birthplace. The 15thC almshouses adjoining the school retain their original function as homes for the aged. Turn left into Old Town. Ahead on the left is Hall's Croft, possibly Stratford's finest Tudor building. Old Town Place (opposite) is a fine early-18thC private house, complete with gas lamps. Ahead to the left is Old Town Croft, another classic black-and-white Tudor property. Continue ahead to Holy Trinity church (see **STRATFORD-WHAT TO SEE**) and see the warning inscribed on Shakespeare's tomb:

GOOD FREND FOR JESUS SAKE FORBEARE TO DIGG THE DUST ENCLOASED HEARE. BLESE (blessed) BE YE MAN YT (that) SPARES THE STONES AND CURST BE HE YT MOVES MY BONES.

Leave the church and after a few yards turn right into the riverside gardens. Ahead is the Brass Rubbing Centre (1000-1800 April-Sep., 1100-1600 Sat., Sun. only, Oct.-Mar.). Rejoin Southern Lane and the Royal Shakespeare Theatre (RST) is straight ahead (see **A-Z**). Beyond the RST are the lovely Bancroft Gardens, a favourite place to feed the ducks and swans. In the far corner is the Gower Memorial, the largest and most impressive Shakespeare memorial in Stratford. It was unveiled in 1888 and comprises a life-size statue of the Bard and statues of Hamlet (representing philosophy), Lady Macbeth (tragedy), Falstaff (comedy) and Prince Hal (history). A fitting end to the walk.

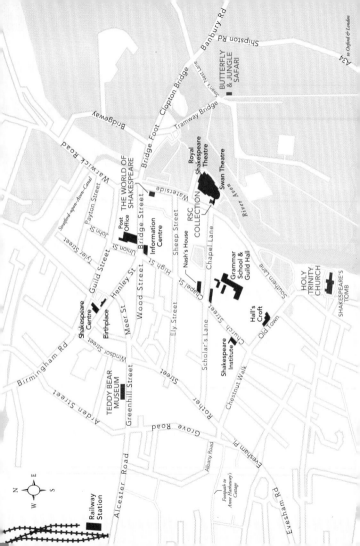

What to See

BUTTERFLY JUNGLE & SAFARI Swan's Nest Lane.

❏ 1000-1800 summer, 1000-dusk winter. ❏ £2.50, senior citizen, child
£1.75, family £6 (Mar.-Nov.); £2, senior citizen, child £1.30 (Dec.-Feb.).
*This is claimed to be the largest butterfly farm in Europe and is set in a
steamy, tropical hothouse. Once in, you'll be ducking and dodging the
brilliantly coloured inhabitants fluttering all around you. 'Insect City' is a
fine, flesh-creeping display which includes giant spiders. See* **Children**.

HOLY TRINITY CHURCH Old Town.

❏ 0830-1800 Mon.-Sat. (summer), 0830-1600 winter; 1400-1700 Sun.
❏ Free. Chancel (Shakespeare's tomb) 40p donation.
*This fine 13th-16thC church is famous as the Bard's last resting place.
Next to his grave are those of his wife, Anne, his daughter, Susanna, and
in-laws, John Hall and Thomas Nash. Above is a brightly coloured mon-
ument (1623) with his authentic likeness. See also his christening font.*

RSC COLLECTION The Swan Theatre, Waterside.

❏ 0915-2000 Mon.-Sat., 1200-1700 Sun.; closes 1600 Sun. (Nov.-Mar.).
❏ £1.50, concessions, child £1.
*A remarkable collection of over 1000 pieces of RSC memorabilia (props,
costumes, paintings and stagecraft) imaginatively and very informally
displayed. An Aladdin's cave for fans. See* **Royal Shakespeare Theatre**.

TEDDY BEAR MUSEUM Greenhill St.

❏ 0930-1800. ❏ £1.75, child under 15 85p.
*This cosy museum in an Elizabethan house is a treat for children of all
ages and serious teddy bear collectors. Antique teddies, unusual bears
and a Hall of Fame including, a Steiff 1903 original, Winnie the Pooh,
Paddington and the original Fozzie Bear. See* **Children**.

THE WORLD OF SHAKESPEARE Waterside.

❏ 0930-1700. Performances every 30 min.
❏ £2.25, concessions, child 6-16 £1.75, family £5.
*25 life-size tableaux combine with dramatic sound and light effects to
take you back to Elizabethan times. Scenes include bear-baiting, the
Plague and royal celebrations. The show lasts 25 min.*

Butterfly Jungle & Safari, Stratford

Abingdon: 5 miles south of Oxford. Pop: 29,000. Market day Mon. This thriving market town is famous for its classic picture-postcard river setting and its abbey, formerly one of the six richest in Britain. Go through the town, beneath the Abbey gateway, and you are in the heart of the historic centre. Carry on to your left and in lovely Abbey Mill Lane you will find the entrance to the domestic buildings which are all that remain of the Abbey (1400-1800 April-Sep., 1400-1600 Tue.-Sun., Oct.-Mar. 50p, child 10p). The Upper Reaches Hotel was built on the site of the monastic watermill and some of the ancient stone wheels can be seen in the terrace gardens. Straight ahead is the Old Gaol, built in 1812 and now holding a leisure centre, the TIC (Tourist Information Centre) and a riverside garden café. Enquire at the TIC about riverside walks and don't miss the view from the bridge (100 yards to the right from the Old Gaol). The church across the river is St. Helen's, built in the 14thC. Both this and the 12thC church of St. Nicholas, by the Abbey gateway, are well worth a visit.
The other glory of the town is the 17thC Old County Hall. Its lower colonnade provides part-shelter for the market, while the upper part houses a local museum (1300-1700 Tue.-Sun., April-Oct.; 1200-1600 Tue.-Sun., Nov.-Mar. 10p).

Accommodation: If you want to stay in Oxford or Stratford during the summer season you should try to book well in advance but if you turn up with nowhere booked the TIC (Tourist Information Centre; see **A-Z**) will help you (there is a small booking fee).
Bed & Breakfasts (B&B), boarding houses and guesthouses are the cheapest lodgings, aside from camping and hostels. Pick up the *B&B Touring Map* for the Heart of Britain (the name of the local tourist-board area) which recommends establishments in Oxfordshire and Stratford for £14.50 or less per person per night (based on twin occupancy). These are often modest private houses but may also be working farms or listed buildings (i.e. of historical or architectural interest). All establishments listed by the tourist boards conform to minimum standards and range from the simply 'listed' (usually meaning clean and comfortable but with few facilities) to the top-of-the-range five crowns with the most comprehensive facilities and service (although this is not

a measure of luxury). Expect to pay £30-40 (more if over two crowns) per couple per night.

In addition to the tourist boards' crown system, the AA and RAC also rank hotels on a one- to five-star rating depending on facilities and degree of luxury. Expect to pay the following per couple per night for a double room: two stars £40-75, three/four stars £60-90. You can also take away some of the guesswork by buying the Consumer Association's *Good Hotel Guide*, or one of the several *Where to Stay* accommodation guides published by the English Tourist Board (ETB). Depending on your capacity for conviviality, a stay in a pub may well be an excellent way of ensuring that good food, drink and company are close at hand. Prices are usually pitched somewhere between a B&B and a hotel, but beware you're not put in the modern annexe when you choose your 15thC inn!

See **Camping & Caravanning**, **Tourist Information**, **Youth Hostels**.

Alcester: 8 miles west of Stratford. Pop: 5400. Market day Fri. Alcester (pronounced 'Olster') is a small, old-world market town clustered around an 18thC church. Walk round it to see the former 17thC Town Hall, the old hand-loom weavers' workshop building and the splendid half-timbered terrace in Malt Mill Lane. High St also boasts many older properties, and just off it is an attraction for antique hunters, the Malt House Antique Centre, where several dealers have permanent stalls. Nearby is Coughton Court, an Elizabethan house holding a collection of Jacobite relics belonging to the followers of James VII and II and the deposed Stuart monarchy, the most famous of whom is Bonnie Prince Charlie (1400-1800 Sat., Sun., April, Easter Sat.-Thu.; 1400-1800 Tue.-Thu., Sat., Sun., Bank Holiday Mon., May-Sep.; 1400-1700 Sat., Sun., Oct. £2.20, child £1.10, family £6.10). Ragley Hall is also near here (see **STRATFORD-HOUSES, CASTLES & PARKS**).

All Souls College, Oxford: All Souls accepts only fellows (see **Oxford University & Colleges**). These are often highly distinguished in their fields and consequently All Souls is the most prestigious of Oxford's colleges in terms of its academic reputation. It was founded in 1483 as a memorial to all the souls of those killed in the Hundred Years' War between France and England (fought intermittently from 1337-1453). The magnificent architecture includes one of the city's finest chapels, dating from the 15thC. Original features include the stained glass in the antechapel, a fine hammer-beam oak roof and a beautiful stone reredos. Famous members include Sir Christopher Wren and T. E. Lawrence (of Arabia). See **OXFORD-UNIVERSITY 1**.

Ashmolean Museum, Oxford: This was England's first public museum, opened in 1683. The present (second) neo-Grecian building dates from 1845 and holds one of the country's most acclaimed provincial collections of art and antiquities. The latter range from the tiny 9thC Saxon Alfred Jewel through the fruits of excavations from Knossos and Egyptian mummies to a startling giant figure of Bodhisattva presiding over the Eastern Art section. Paintings and drawings from British, Impressionist, Pre-Raphaelite and Italian Renaissance schools include many famous old masters. Other highlights are Nubian art, Asian art, Islamic and Japanese ceramics, and European stringed instruments. One of the most intriguing displays is the Tradescant Room, featuring curiosities from around the world and the remnants of Elias Ashmole's original collection. These include Guy Fawkes' lantern and Oliver Cromwell's death mask.

There is too much to see in one visit but admission is free so you can come back as often as you wish. See **OXFORD-WHAT TO SEE 1**.

Banbury: 23 miles north of Oxford, 21 miles southwest of Stratford. Pop: 38,000. Famous for the old nursery rhyme *Ride a Cock Horse to Banbury Cross*, the modern-day town is rather more prosaic and the meaning of the rhyme is lost in the mists of time. Its traffic-choked cross is a 19thC replica and its other claim to fame, the Banbury Cake Shop, sadly was demolished in the 1950s. You can still buy cakes, however (from Malcolm's by the cross), and see the original shop oven in the small, colourful museum, also by the cross, where the TIC (Tourist Information Centre) is located (1000-1700 Mon.-Sat., April-Sep.; 1000-1630 Tue.-Sat., Oct.-Mar.). See also the church of St. Mary's with the 'pepperpot' tower.

The Barringtons: See **OXFORD-EXCURSION 1**.

Bicycle & Motorcycle Hire: Oxford is a city of cyclists, and cycle lanes and cycle parking are abundant. Stratford and the Cotswolds are also ideal for cycling though you may wish to buy an Ordnance Survey map to show you where the steepest hills are. Be careful cycling in town centres and also on single-track roads where hedgerows may

obscure your vision. Always lock your bike when you leave it unattended. You can take a bike free of charge on some British Rail services but on others you will have to pay £3.

Bicycle hire shops around the area are as follows:

Oxford – Broadrib Ltd, Market St: 3-speed £9/first week, £5 each subsequent week (min. one-week hire), £20 deposit; Pennyfarthing, 5 George St: 3-speed £9/first week, £6 each subsequent week, £5/day, £20 deposit. Ladies' 5-speed/gents' 10-speed £15/week, £40 deposit.

Stratford – Clarke's Cycle Shop (Esso garage), Guild St: 3/5/10-speed £4/day, £18/week, £50 deposit.

There is no motorcycle hire in either Oxford or Stratford due to insurance difficulties.

Blenheim Palace: 'An Italian palace in an English park without incongruity' was how Sir Winston Churchill described Blenheim. He was born here in 1874 and in 1908 proposed to Clementine Hozier in the Temple of Diana in the grounds. The house was built between the years 1705-22 for John Churchill, 1st Duke of Marlborough, in recognition of his great national victory over the French at the Battle of Blenheim in 1704. The most obvious reminder of this is the 134-ft-tall

Column of Victory towering in the distance. The Palace is best approached through Woodstock (see **A-Z**). As you pass the entrance archway, the Capability Brown/Vanbrugh vista of lake, Grand Bridge and house has been described as 'the finest view in England'. It is undoubtedly a masterpiece of landscape gardening. The Palace, part-country house, part-national monument and part-citadel, is no less impressive. A guided tour moves you through the striking Great Hall, The Churchill Exhibition, lavish State Rooms, the outstanding Long Library (183 ft) containing over 10,000 volumes, and finishes in the chapel, with pompous tombs fit for royalty. The 2200 acres of grounds boast a formal Italian garden and water terraces (you can take afternoon tea here) and the more natural charms of an arboretum and a grand cascade (a picturesque small waterfall). For children there is a butterfly house, an adventure playground and a model railway. Allow a full day to explore Blenheim, taking in Woodstock (see **A-Z**) and Churchill's grave, two miles south at Bladon. See **OXFORD-HOUSES & PARKS**, **Tours**.

Boats: Boating is a pleasant way to see another side of the country around Oxford, Stratford and the Cotswolds, and there are several options to suit anyone's level of expertise. If you fancy a do-it-yourself trip on the water, consider taking out a rowing boat or a punt. A punt is an open, narrow, flat-bottomed craft with square ends, designed for use in shallow waters and propelled by a long pole (or punt) which is pushed against the riverbed and which also serves as the rudder. However, it is not as easy as it looks and should not be attempted by non-swimmers. Punting on the Cherwell is easier than on the Thames or Avon as motorboats are prohibited. In Oxford you can hire punts and rowing boats from Folly Bridge, Magdalen Bridge and Cherwell Boathouse. In Stratford, boats (punts, canoes and rowing boats) can be hired from Rose's Boathouse (£2 per person per hour), Swan's Nest Lane or by the ferry on Waterside. Prices average £5-6 per boat per hour; a deposit of £10-25 and proof of identity may be required. For the less experienced or less confident an organized boat trip may be a better alternative. In Oxford Salter Bros. at Folly Bridge run daily trips to Abingdon (see **A-Z**) (mid-May-early Sep.) and will hire boats for parties (min. 12 people), while in Stratford there are regular 30-min trips along the Avon from Bancroft Gardens (£1.50, child 75p). Finally, a boating holiday is an excellent way to see unspoilt country-side and moorings are plentiful. Blakes Holidays offer both narrow boats (barge-like canal craft) and conventional cruisers for boating holidays, starting from Abingdon, Oxford and Stratford.

Bodleian Library, Oxford: This world-famous establishment has its origins in the original collection begun by Duke Humfrey and completed in 1488. His library still survives and is the highlight of a Bodleian tour. By 1556, however, the collection was lost and it was Sir Thomas Bodley who in 1598 started the library that exists today. The Schools Quad. was built in 1619 to house the burgeoning collection and the names above the doors indicate the disciplines formerly stud-ied there. It is now administration offices and reading rooms. Inside the Quad. is the 15thC Divinity School, a beautiful fan-vaulted room which was the original University lecture room. By 1789 the Schools Quad. building was full and in 1860 the Radcliffe Camera was taken over as library space. This, too, was soon filled and today the collection of over five million volumes, which occupies over 84 miles of shelving, is mostly housed in the New Library (built in 1939) on the opposite side of Broad St (not open to the public). It comprises 11 storeys, seven of which are below ground, and has an area six times that of the Radcliffe Camera. See **OXFORD-UNIVERSITY 3**, **OXFORD-WALK 1**, **OXFORD-WALK 2**.

Bourton-on-the-Water: 26 miles west of Oxford, 19 miles south of Stratford. Pop: 4000. This large, pretty village really is on the water, its length bisected by the shallow River Windrush which is crisscrossed by five small, ornamental bridges. Unfortunately, at the height of the season its charm all but vanishes under hordes of day-trippers and fast-food vendors but it is worth a visit at any time for the two first-class attractions of Birdland and the Cotswold Motor Museum. At Birdland the penguins invariably steal the show but they are just a few of the 320 colourful species at this well-designed collection, laid out around waterways full of voracious trout (1030-1800, April-Oct.; 1000-1600, Nov.-Mar. £2.50, senior citizen £2, child 4-14 £1.80). The Cotswold Motor Museum is a wonderfully nostalgic look back over the decades of carefree motoring and will delight even those with little interest in cars. Vintage motors jostle for space with over 7000 complementary period pieces and the overall impression is of having entered a huge, time-warped garage complete with 1920s music. The Village Life exhibition, set in the same charming 18thC mill, partners the museum perfectly with an atmospheric arrangement of bygones, including a reconstruction of the old village shop (1000-1800, Feb.-Nov. Joint ticket £1, child under 15 55p, family £3).

The Cotswold Perfumery, featuring an audio-visual introduction, a per-fumed garden and 'nose-on' exhibits is different and fun (0900-1700. 80p, concessions and child 70p). Other attractions are the Model Village (0900-1800 summer; 1000-1600 winter. 85p, senior citizen 75p, child 65p) and the Model Railway (1100-1730 April-Sep.; 1100-1730 Sat., Sun., Oct.-Mar. £1, senior citizen 90p, child 4-15 80p). See also the church and explore the backstreets where, on Clapton Row, you will find The Bourton Pottery with potters often at work. Try the Small Talk Tea Room for something light or The Rose Tree for a meal. The TIC (Tourist Information Centre) is in Brasshopper in High St. Three miles away on the A 436 to Cheltenham is Folly Farm, another fine place for children, with over 150 breeds of waterfowl (1100-1800 Mar.-Oct.; 1100-1600 Nov.-Feb. £2, senior citizen £1.30, child £1). See **OXFORD-EXCURSION 1**, **Children**.

Broadway: 14 miles south of Stratford. Pop: 2800. This immaculate large village straddles the broad, curving High St which gives the place its name. In the 17thC Broadway was a major staging centre boasting 33 pubs. The outstanding survivor is The Lygon Arms, now one of England's most famous country hotels. Look inside and see its lounges and shop. Goblets Wine Bar, part of the building, is a good option for lunch. Broadway exudes a strong aura of wealth – there are no 'attrac-tions' here (the fine Broadway Tower Country Park is close by; see **STRATFORD-EXCURSION 2**) and it is doubtful whether you will find many bargains in its galleries and antique shops. For many people, however, the look of the place is enough and the harmony of the lovely golden-stone buildings does take some beating. Walk beyond the green and turn left up Church St into beautiful countryside. Go past the 'new' Victorian church as far as the lovely old 13thC church. Try Tisanes for afternoon tea. The TIC (Tourist Information Centre) is in Cotswold Court and is open in summer only. See **STRATFORD-EXCURSION 1**.

Burford: 18 miles west of Oxford. Pop: 1500. The view looking down the steep, wide, 15th-16thC High St of Burford is one of the

Cotswolds' great sights. The town owed its medieval prosperity to wool (see **A-Z**), then became a major staging point and it retains some fine pubs. The oldest and finest of these is The Lamb which is beautifully decorated in a 'country antique' style and has a lovely garden. The best way to see Burford itself is by guided tour, setting off from the corner of Sheep St and High St (1430 Sat., Sun., May-Oct. 50p, child 20p) or follow the *Burford Trail* leaflet (available from the Tourist Information Centre in Sheep St, 20p). This takes you up Sheep St, past the garden of *The Countryman* magazine (free), then right into Priory Lane and across High St to see the splendid monuments in the church. Follow Church Lane into Guildenford and back to High St via Witney St. The 16thC Tolsey building where the Guild of Merchants once met is now a small local museum (1430-1730 April-Oct. 30p). See **OXFORD-EXCURSION 1**.

Buses: Oxford's main station is at Gloucester Green. Oxford Citylink no. 190 runs nonstop to Victoria Station, London, every 20-30 min daily. The average journey time is 1 hr 40 min. A day return (from Oxford; prices are higher if you buy your ticket in London) is £3, child under 16 £2.75; period return £5, child £3. For details of Citylink services, tel: 0865-248190. A similar service is run by 'The Oxford Tube' with free refreshments and costs £3.95 for a day return to Victoria,

£2.95 for other London stops, £5.95 for a period return, £4.95 for other stops. For general bus and coach enquiries, tel: 0865-711312.
Stratford's main station is at Bridge Foot. National Express run an hourly service daily to Victoria, tel: 021-6224373. Return fare Sat.-Thu. £10, Fri. £13.25. For local services, tel: 0788-535555. There are two buses per day between Oxford and Stratford with fares of £3.40 return, £2.50 single. See **Transport**.

Camping & Caravanning: There are good facilities for caravanning and camping around Oxford and the Cotswolds, and some of the sites are noted below. All have showers, electric hook-up points and a shop, and are open April-Oct. unless stated otherwise. Prices per pitch per night range from £5-7. This is not a complete list of sites: for a more extensive range, see *FHG Guide to Caravan & Camping Holidays* (£1.95), *Caravans & Chalet Park Guide* (£2.50), *Where to Stay Camping & Caravan Parks* (£3.99), or ask at the TIC (Tourist Information Centre; see **A-Z**). You may be able to rent a caravan or camping vehicle from a car-hire firm.
Oxford – Camping International, Abingdon Rd: 1.5 miles from Oxford, no hook-ups, open all year, tel: 0865-246551; Cassington Mill: 6 miles from Oxford, no shop, tel: 0865-881081; Hardwick Parks, Standlake: 9 miles from Oxford, caravans (3) for hire, water sports, tel: 0865-300501; Lincoln Farm Park, Standlake: caravans (2) for hire, water sports, excellent standard of facilities, tel: 0865-300239; Diamond Farm, Bletchington, tel: 0865-50909.
Stratford – Dodwell Park: 2 miles from Stratford, tel: 0789-204957.
Cotswolds – Cotswold View Park, Charlbury: 7 miles from Chipping Norton, excellent standard of facilities, tel: 0608-810314; Folly Farm: 2 miles from Bourton-on-the-Water, open all year, tel: 0451-20285.

Chastleton House: See STRATFORD-EXCURSION 3.

Chemists: Both Oxford and Stratford have a 'rota service' whereby at least one chemist stays open late and after that they are on call. See the TIC (Tourist Information Centre; see **A-Z**) window for details.

Children: Although the colleges and the Shakespearean Properties may be dull fare for youngsters there is still plenty to do. The following are recommended:

Stratford: Teddy Bear Museum (see **STRATFORD-WHAT TO SEE**); Butterfly Jungle & Safari (see **STRATFORD-WHAT TO SEE**); Warwick Castle (see **A-Z**). Oxford: church-tower views; University Museum (see **OXFORD-WHAT TO SEE 2**); Pitt Rivers Museum (see **OXFORD-WHAT TO SEE 2**); the ice-rink. Cotswolds: any country, wildlife or farm park; Bourton-on-the-Water (see **A-Z**) ; Winchcombe Railway Museum (see **Winchcombe**); Snowshill Manor (see **A-Z**). Boat trips anywhere go down well (see **Boats**) and many country houses (Blenheim, Ragley, etc.) also provide play and picnic areas for children. Note that some guesthouses and hotels do not welcome young children.

There is a baby-changing room in Oxford at Debenhams and at the Bridge Foot multi-storey car park. See **Events**, **Public Houses**.

Chipping Campden: 39 miles northwest of Oxford, 12 miles south of Stratford. Pop: 2000. This was one of the greatest of the Cotswold wool towns of the 13th and 14thC (see **Wool**) and that era of prosperity is attested by the impressive 15thC church and the Woolstaplers Hall, built c.1340. The latter now holds the TIC (Tourist Information Centre) and an excellent, diverse museum which, as well as its wool-history exhibits, contains a Victorian parachute and other interesting items (1100-1800 April-Oct. £1, child 50p). Almost opposite is the 14thC house of William Grevel, one of England's greatest medieval wool merchants, who is buried in the church a short walk away. The most sketched and photographed building in town is the open-air Market

Hall, built in 1627, with a gloriously uneven stone floor. Have a drink and a bite at The King's Arms hotel or The Noel Arms. Robert Dover's Cotswold Games ('the Cotswolds Olympicks') take place just outside the village at Dover Hill (see **Events**). They comprise a parade, morris men, fireworks and the Games themselves – tug of war, welly wanging (hurling a Wellington boot), climbing a greasy pole and other unlikely pursuits (£1.50, child 50p)! For many people this is the best all-round town in the Cotswolds and it makes an excellent overnight stay to extend an excursion. See **STRAT-FORD-EXCURSION 2**.

Christ Church College, Oxford

Christ Church College, Oxford: Henry VIII founded Christ Church in 1546, taking over the building of the college from his disgraced chancellor Cardinal Wolsey. Parts of the cathedral and chapter house, however, go back to the 12th or 13thC priory of St. Frideswide, the patron saint of Oxford. The college's centrepiece is the landmark Tom Tower (named after its bell, Great Tom) built by Sir Christopher Wren in 1682. However, the pride and joy of the college is its hall, the largest and most impressive in Oxford, built under Wolsey. As you ascend the 17thC hall staircase look up at its fan-tracery roof. The hall itself boasts a magnificent, richly carved hammer-beam roof. Members' portraits include many of the 13 British prime ministers who have attended here and also Charles L. Dodgson who in 1865, under the pen name of Lewis Carroll, wrote *Alice in Wonderland* here, dedicated to Alice Liddell, the Dean's daughter (see **OXFORD-WALK 3**). Other famous members include William Penn, John Wesley and W. H. Auden. The portraits include works by Reynolds, Gainsborough, Millais and Graham Sutherland. Tour the cathedral clockwise and note the lovely 17thC 'Jonah' window; the simple grave of St. Frideswide and the adjacent rare wooden watching chamber (where the monks would sit on guard to protect the holy relics); the beautiful 15thC vaulted roof of the choir; the monuments to Royalist soldiers killed in the English Civil War (1642-48); and the 14thC Becket window. The Picture Gallery is a dull, modern block but it holds a superb collection of old masters' paintings, including works by Veronese, Tintoretto, Van Dyck and Reynolds, and drawings by Dürer, Rembrandt and Rubens. A few yards from here lies Christ Church Meadow, a remarkable pastoral scene, given its proximity to the city centre, with grazing cattle amid acres of unspoiled countryside bordered by the Thames and Cherwell. See **OXFORD-UNIVERSITY 1**, **OXFORD-WALK 1**.

Cotswolds: The area takes its name from the range of hills stretching southwest from Chipping Campden and Broadway in the north to Witney, Lechlade, Tetbury and Wotton-under-Edge in the south. The hills in turn were named after the Saxon words *cotes* (sheep fold) and *wold* (bare hill). Much of England's medieval wealth was built up here on the great flocks of sheep and the export of their fleeces but the area is now famous for its outstanding natural beauty and its golden-stone buildings. See **Wool**.

Disabled People: It is always advisable to 'phone ahead to request assistance, ascertain particular difficulties, check lifts are working, etc. before visiting places. As many of the buildings and attractions in this area are fairly ancient, wheelchair access can be a problem. Recommended places with reasonable access include the following:
Oxford: Ashmolean Museum (see **OXFORD-WHAT TO SEE 1**, **A-Z**); University Museum (see **OXFORD-WHAT TO SEE 2**); New College (see **OXFORD-UNIVERSITY 2**, **A-Z**); Christ Church College (steep ramps; see **OXFORD-UNIVERSITY 1**, **A-Z**); Magdalen College (enquire for route avoiding steps; see **OXFORD-UNIVERSITY 2**, **A-Z**); Blenheim Palace (steep ramps; see **OXFORD-HOUSES & PARKS**, **A-Z**).
Stratford: Holy Trinity church (see **STRATFORD-WHAT TO SEE**); Charlecote House (see **STRATFORD-HOUSES, CASTLES & PARKS**); Mary Arden's House (see **STRATFORD-SHAKESPEARE**); The Shakespeare Centre (see **STRATFORD-SHAKESPEARE**).
There are wheelchair toilets in Oxford at Westgate Centre, Gloucester Green bus station, Speedwell St (off St. Aldate's) and in Stratford at Bridge Foot, The Water Rat, Waterside (opposite Bancroft Gardens) and in the multi-storey car parks at Windsor St and Rother St.

Eating Out: There are numerous good places to eat out in Oxford serving high-quality food to both locals and tourists. Many establishments in Stratford and the Cotswolds, however, just cater for tourists, with a noticeable decline in imagination and standards. The cheapest places to eat well in a good atmosphere are often pubs, most serving bar food between 1200-1400 and 1900-2100 Mon.-Sat. Quality can vary enormously but as the food is often on display at least you can see what you are getting. Aside from the establishments recommended (see **OXFORD-RESTAURANTS**, **STRATFORD-RESTAURANTS**) you may also like to try the following:
Oxford: Elizabeth Restaurant (French/international; Expensive); Michel's Brasserie (French; Moderate); The Paddyfield (Chinese; Moderate); Jamals (Indian; Moderate); Cita Tapas (Spanish; Inexpensive-Moderate);

and Go Dutch (Dutch; Inexpensive). Gourmets with fat wallets should note that Raymond Blanc's Le Manoir aux Quat' Saisons is just seven miles from Oxford at Great Milton. For takeaways try the Cowley Rd Indian restaurants or the locally famous Brett's Burgers by the railway station. Recommended daytime coffee and snack stops include the following: The Nosebag; St. Aldate's Coffee Shop; The Wykeham Coffee Shop; Debenhams; and Baedeker's.

Stratford: try Fatty Arbuckle's (bistro; Moderate) and Hussain's (Indian; Moderate), while a recommended coffee stop is Dealer's Den (Antique Centre, Ely St).

The price categories in the **RESTAURANTS** pages and above are based on a three-course meal with a bottle of house wine and coffee for two people and are as follows:

Inexpensive	£15-25
Moderate	£25-40
Expensive	£40-70

Emergency Numbers: Casualty Departments:
John Radcliffe Hospital, Oxford, tel: 0865-64711
South Warwickshire Hospital, Warwick, tel: 0926-495321

Dover's Games

Events:

Last week in February: Torpids, Oxford, the college rowing races held on the Thames (see **Sports**).

Weekend closest to 23 April: Shakespeare's Birthday celebrations, Stratford, with a floral procession from his Birthplace (see **STRATFORD-SHAKESPEARE**) to Holy Trinity church, his last resting place (see **STRATFORD-WHAT TO SEE**).

1 May: May Day, Oxford, when Magdalen College Choir sing from Magdalen Tower at 0600. It gets very crowded and you will have to be there by 0530 to get within earshot. This is followed by morris dancing and musicians playing in Radcliffe Sq.

May Day Bank Holiday: 'Fun in the Parks', Oxford, featuring outdoor music, dance, drama and children's events. This is the first of six such days throughout the summer; other fixed dates are the first Sat. in July and the second Sat. in Sep.

Late May: Eights Week (Wed.-Sat. in the 5th week of Trinity term), Oxford, the inter-collegiate rowing races (see **Sports**).

Late May/early June: (weekend after the Spring Bank Hol.) Dover's Games, Chipping Campden (see **Chipping Campden**); Artsweek, Oxford and Oxfordshire, Britain's largest visual-arts festival, with exhibitions, demonstrations, etc. at dozens of venues.

Mid-June: Woodstock carnival (takes place in early evening).

Third Saturday in June: Stratford regatta.

Mid-late June: Encaenia, Oxford (see **Oxford University & Colleges**).

First week in July: Henley Royal Regatta (see **Henley-on-Thames**).

Second week in July: Henley Festival of Music and the Arts, comprising three days of classical music, jazz, opera and recitals, with exhibitions of paintings and sculpture (see **Henley-on-Thames**).

Last two weeks in July and first week in August: Stratford festival and carnival with artistic, musical and literary events.

Mid-August: Oxford regatta; Abingdon regatta.

Last Monday in August: (Summer Bank Hol.) Water Games, Bourton-on-the-Water, featuring an eccentric game of football through the River Windrush.

Early September: (Mon. and Tue. after the first Sun. following 1 Sep.) St. Giles' Fair, Oxford, a large funfair.

12 October: Stratford Mop Fair, a traditional ox-roast and funfair.

A full list of Oxford events is available from the TIC (Tourist Information Centre; see **A-Z**).

Evesham: 14 miles west of Stratford. Pop: 15,000. Market day Sat. This pretty town set on the Avon is famous as the market centre for the Vale of Evesham's fruit-growing industry. It has retained its old-world appeal, most notably in its Market Place buildings and in its ruined Abbey precincts. The Old Almonry, a former pilgrims' lodgings at the Abbey Gate, is now a local museum (1000-1700 Mon.-Sat., 1400-1700 Sun., Good Fri.-Sep. 40p, child free) and also houses the TIC (Tourist Information Centre).

Charlecote Park

Excursions: In addition to the five excursions in the blue-banded pages, the following days out are recommended:
London (56 miles from Oxford, 96 from Stratford; see Collins Traveller City Guide to London); Bath (70 miles from Oxford, 74 from Stratford), Britain's most famous spa town with fascinating Roman Baths and Museum plus many other sights; Cheltenham (41 miles from Oxford, 31 from Stratford), another elegant Regency spa town, much quieter than Bath, with a famous promenade; Stroud (48 miles from Oxford, 45 from Stratford), another important wool town; Cirencester (35 miles from Oxford, 40 from Stratford), once the largest provincial town in Britain.

Falconry: The sport of medieval and Tudor royalty is now an exciting and educational tourist attraction at Batsford Park (Cotswold Falconry Centre; see **STRATFORD-EXCURSION 3**), Charlecote Park (see **STRATFORD-HOUSES, CASTLES & PARKS**) and Mary Arden's House (see **STRATFORD-SHAKESPEARE**). Falcons, hawks, eagles and owls are put through their paces, and this includes a high-speed game of cat-and-mouse to see if they can snatch away the swinging lure (a piece of meat on the end of a rope) before the falconer sees their approach and whips it away from them. The show at Batsford is particularly recommended.

Gargoyles: See **Grotesques & Gargoyles**.

Grotesques & Gargoyles: The former is a bizarre 16thC decorative style in which bits of human, animal and plant form are distorted and mixed together, while the latter is a grotesque face or creature used as a waterspout. Their unpleasant appearances were once thought to be a deterrent to evil spirits. Look up almost anywhere in the old parts of Oxford and you will see them staring back down at you from the tops of the buildings. New College (see **OXFORD-UNIVERSITY 2**, **A–Z**) and Magdalen (see **OXFORD-UNIVERSITY 2**, **A–Z**) have particularly good examples.

Guides: Guide Friday Ltd is the main tour operator and guide-services company in both Oxford and Stratford. The company's professionalism and knowledge is exemplary and an hour on an open-top bus with one of their witty, irreverent guides is great entertainment. The only real way to see Oxford, however, is on foot. The official tour, lasting 2 hr, departs from the TIC (Tourist Information Centre; see **A-Z**) regularly throughout the day in summer (reduced service operates in winter). Buy your ticket in advance (£2.40, child £1) at the TIC. All tours are conducted by 'blue-badge' guides who have passed a rigorous, nationally recognized training course. Tours are also led by university students, and while their guiding skills may be more variable, their inside knowledge is unimpeachable and they may get you into places otherwise off-limits to the public. These leave regularly from the University church on the High St, cost around £2-£2.40 for 60-90 min (children often go free) and, in case of rain, the guides may even lend you an umbrella! Stratford also runs official 'blue-badge' guided tours, lasting 1 hr 30 min, with regular departures from the TIC (summer only, £1.50, child 60p).

If you would like to go rambling in the Cotswolds with an experienced warden, pick up a *Guided Walks in the Cotswolds* leaflet from the TIC or tel: 0452-425674. See **Orientation**, **Tours**.

Henley-on-Thames: 23 miles south of Oxford. Pop: 11,000. Market day Thu. This prosperous small town is world-famous for the Royal Regatta, one of the unmissable events in the aristocratic English social calendar. Jazz bands play, international oarsmen scull, champagne corks pop and everyone has an awfully, awfully nice time. Following hard on its heels is the Festival of Music and the Arts, combining music, art, theatre and food in a riverside setting. See **Events**.

Magdalen College, Oxford: (pronounced 'Maudlin'). The terms 'gracious' and 'spacious' are the most overworked adjectives when it comes to describing Magdalen. Its cloisters are some of the largest and finest in Oxford and evoke an eerie medieval-religious atmosphere. Magdalen has one of the best collections of grotesques and gargoyles (see **A-Z**) in Oxford, particularly around the cloisters. Take the tour to see the hall, built 1474, with its original linenfold panelling, its (modern) timber roof and its portraits of the mighty, including Cardinal

Wolsey who was, by tradition, responsible for Magdalen's famous tower. Attend Evensong to hear the famous choir (see **Events**) in the 15thC chapel with its fine wood carving and its stone reredos, and don't miss the Deerparks and Waterwalks, like Christ Church Meadow, virgin countryside only a few yards from throbbing city traffic. A 20-min walk round the Meadow can be extended by taking in Addison's Walk. Famous members include Oscar Wilde, John Betjeman and Dudley Moore. See **OXFORD-UNIVERSITY 2**, **OXFORD-WALK 1**.

Markets: Traditional, open-air markets are the original *raison d'être* for many rural English towns and the markets that survive today are their direct descendants. They are colourful and lively and are as good to watch as to buy from. You may be able to haggle at a goods market, but you'll get short shrift at a food market: if you want a bargain, wait until late in the day when the prices tumble. There are general markets in Oxford on Wed. (0900-!ate afternoon) at Gloucester Green and in Stratford on Fri. morning at Rother St. For other market days see individual town and village listings. See **Shopping**.

Merton College, Oxford: Founded in 1264, this is one of Oxford's oldest colleges. Its chapel is claimed to be the oldest in the city, dating from 1297, with its elaborate tower added in 1451. See the impressive memorial to former member Sir Thomas Bodley (founder of the Bodleian Library; see **A-Z**) and the original choir windows. The Old Library, built in 1378, contains many original fittings, ancient books and Chaucer's astrolabe (an early astronomical and navigational device). If you are on a guided walking tour with a former Merton student you may also get to see the Real Tennis Court, normally closed to the public. Famous members include Lord Randolph Churchill, T. S. Eliot, Robert Morley and Kris Kristofferson. See **OXFORD-UNIVERSITY 2**.

Music: Oxford has a lively pop-rock scene, with several venues host-ing good local bands regularly. The best venue is probably The Old Fire Station Café which puts on consistently good blues, rock, pop and indie bands (Mon.-Sat. £4-5; see **OXFORD-CITY PUBS**). The Jericho Tavern in Walton St in the Jericho district is a less salubrious setting but with a long history of promoting similar music almost every night (c.£4). Top bands regularly play the Apollo Theatre, George St (c.£8). Oxford's premier folk-music club meets at The Port Mahon, St. Clement's St (2000 Fri. £1) and there are also folk nights at The Bullingdon Arms, Cowley Rd (Wed.) and the Prince of Wales, Church Way, Iffley (2100 Wed.). Jazz buffs should head for The Turl bar at The Mitre on Turl St (Fri. £2). The major classical music venues are The Holywell Music Room (which has been going strong for over 240 years) and the Sheldonian Theatre, reputedly the most uncomfortable venue in town, so be sure to take a cushion. The Holywell stages a series of 'coffee concerts' mid-Feb.-early June (1115 Sun. £3.50, concessions and child £2.50, includes coffee). Other regular venues are the Apollo Theatre and Christ Church cathedral. The highlight of the season is the Fireworks Concert at Radley College in late July.

Music at Oxford deal with classical music bookings, tel: 0865-864056. Tickets in Oxford, based in the TIC (Tourist Information Centre; see **A-Z**), sell tickets for the theatre and concerts in Oxford, Stratford and London. Note that there will be a double booking charge added to the face value of tickets bought from here for London shows to cover both the fees of a London agency and Tickets in Oxford.

Stratford has few music venues: The Swan Theatre occasionally features jazz, folk and big band, and the Civic Hall in Rother St hosts classical and light music from time to time. Near Coventry (19 miles away) is the excellent University of Warwick Arts Centre which claims to be Britain's largest provincial performance- and visual-arts complex. Pick up a programme from the TIC. Birmingham (24 miles away) is a major entertainment centre. See **Events**, **What's On**.

New College, Oxford: Renowned for its architectural beauty, New College was founded in 1379 by William of Wykeham, Bishop of Winchester and Chancellor of England. His crosier (bishop's staff) can still be seen in the chapel which is also notable for its art treasures and carved stone reredos. The 14thC hall is the oldest in Oxford and retains its early-16thC wooden panelling. Step out to the lovely gardens which are bordered by the old city wall. This is probably the best-preserved and most ancient surviving section, dating from the 12thC. Like Magdalen (see **A-Z**), the cloisters here are very atmospheric, particularly as the light is fading, and at Evensong you will hear some of the city's finest voices. Famous New College members include Tony Benn and John Galsworthy, author of *The Forsyte Saga*. See **OXFORD-UNIVERSITY 2**, **OXFORD-WALK 1**, **Grotesques & Gargoyles**.

Nightlife: As you would expect from a cosmopolitan student city, both music (see **A-Z**) and theatre (see **A-Z**) are well represented in Oxford. There are two mainstream Cannon cinemas in the city centre as well as the Phoenix on Walton Rd and The Penultimate Picture Palace just off Cowley Rd, both of which show cult classics and recent releases. There are a handful of discos and nightclubs (the Tourist Information Centre – see **A-Z** – will provide you with a list), the best of which is Coven II on Oxpens Rd. Stratford's nightlife revolves mostly around the Royal Shakespeare Theatre (see **A-Z**). There is a cinema on Waterside and Celebrities nightclub on Henley St. See **OXFORD-RESTAURANTS**, **STRATFORD-RESTAURANTS**.

Opening Times:

Banks – 0930-1500/1530 Mon.-Fri. Most High St banks in Oxford and Stratford also open 0930-1200 Sat.
Churches – dawn to dusk.
Colleges – most open at least 1400-1700.
Country houses – considerable variation but most open at least on weekend afternoons in summer.
Post Offices – 0900-1730 Mon.-Fri., 0900-1230 Sat.
Pubs – Traditional hours 1100-1430/1500, 1730-2300 Mon.-Sat, 1200-1400, 1900-2230 Sun.; All-day opening 1100-2300 Mon.-Sat., 1200-1500, 1900-2230 Sun.
Shops – 0900-1730 Mon.-Sat. Many tourist shops in popular towns and villages will open on Sun. afternoon in summer.

Orientation: Head straight for the TIC (Tourist Information Centre) and pick up a local map for a few pence. Both Oxford and Stratford are quite compact and can easily be covered on foot. However, it is worth buying a detailed map if you intend touring so that you can avoid the main roads. For the best introduction to both towns take the Guide Friday bus tour, followed by a walking tour. See **Guides**, **Tourist Information**, **Tours**.

Oxford: 56 miles north of London, 40 miles south of Stratford. Pop: 115,000. Although it may not be apparent to the average day-tripper, Oxford is a city with an identity apart from the University and its related tourist industry. Just a couple of miles southeast at Cowley is one of the major manufacturing sites of the giant Rover car group. As the tour guides may tell you, the people who live there are said to regard Oxford centre as Cowley's Latin Quarter! Even before the University arrived Oxford was a thriving market centre and the Normans established it as a military town. St. George's Tower – as old as the Tower of London – is all that remains of the once-impressive Oxford castle. You can see it (though there is no public access) en route to the railway station behind New Rd. Even though many of the colleges are quite well hidden away, the centre of town is dominated by the University and by a busy shopping centre. Thankfully, the abhorrent 'developments' at Queen St and Cornmarket St are balanced by the gracious main thoroughfares of Broad St and High St (known as 'the High'). One of the great things about Oxford for a tourist is its compact nature – you can easily walk from one side of the centre of town to the other in around 20 min. It's worth looking just a little further out, though. To the south, the start of Cowley Rd is an interesting mix of alternative-style, Bohemian-looking shops and ethnic restaurants. Look out for the eccentric Hi-Lo Jamaican Eating House Restaurant and the startling Penultimate Picture Palace cinema. Explore to the north of the centre, passing through the University Parks (see **Walks**) and along the start of Banbury Rd. Some of the heavy Victorian Gothic-revival houses here could be from a Hammer horror film set, but just a little way on the left is the charming, bijou North Parade, a tiny, gentrified row of pubs, restaurants and shops, while a little further to the right is Bardwell

Rd, leading down to the Cherwell Boathouse and the river. You can also take a lovely walk across meadows to the river to the west of the centre (see **OXFORD-WALK 3**), and to the east the countryside is almost equally verdant and pleasant.

Oxford University & Colleges: The University had no formal beginnings and cannot even be dated precisely. Scholars were first heard of in the city before 1200 and the exodus of English students from Paris in 1167 would have encouraged the growth of the first English university. These early students lived in one of 60 halls and studied theology, logic and rhetoric, 'apprenticed' to a master for a term of seven years. Many of the earlier-established colleges were founded by rich and politically powerful bishops and churned out a political and religious elite. Today there are 35 colleges, of which 28 take both undergraduates and graduates. The newest, St. Catherine's, was founded in 1963 and it is also the largest, with over 400 undergraduates. All the main colleges are now co-educational and there are three women-only establishments. To prove that Oxford still produces the elite, one of the women's colleges, Somerville, ranks Margaret Thatcher and Indira Gandhi among its alumni. Undergraduates make up some 9500 of the total Oxford student population of 12,000.

Visitors are often baffled as to the difference between the University and the colleges. Basically, the University acts as a corporate 'holding' body. It sets the examinations (held in the Examination Schools on High St), awards the degrees (in the Sheldonian Theatre) and shares overall administration with the individual colleges. It also owns those facilities

Bodleian Library ceiling

common to the colleges, e.g. the Bodleian Library and the University Parks. The head of the University is the Chancellor. The colleges own and run their own buildings and the college head is known either as the principal, master, warden, rector, dean (at Christ Church) or provost. The teaching and research staff of the colleges are known as fellows or, more popularly, dons, from the Latin *dominus* meaning master or teacher. They are drawn from distinguished scholars (from any university) to take on teaching or research appointments. Students are taught either singly or in small groups, known as tutorials. Undergraduates live initially in the college for a year or two, then move out to a college hostel or lodgings. They are expected to dine in their college hall and used to have to attend chapel daily, but the times have changed. The academic year is less than seven months and is split into three terms: Michaelmas (early Oct.-early Dec.), Hilary (the third week in Jan.-mid Mar.) and Trinity (late April-mid June). Exams are held in May and June and degrees are awarded throughout the year. However, the ceremonial highlight of the year, Encaenia (pronounced 'Ensenior'),

does not directly concern the students. This is the conferring of a limited number of honorary degrees on national and international digni-
taries (see **Events**). But don't be deceived by the pomp and ceremony
and the ancient buildings into thinking that the colleges are museum
pieces with nothing to offer the 20thC: a great many of the leaders of
industry, politics, the arts and sciences in countries all over the world
are graduates of Oxford University.

Of the 35 colleges you should see all the 12 listed in OXFORD-
UNIVERSITY 1, 2, 3 or, if you don't have enough time, try at least to see
the following from that list: All Souls (see **A-Z**), Christ Church (see **A-Z**),
Magdalen (see **A-Z**), Merton (see **A-Z**) and New (see **A-Z**). Most are
open at least 1400-1700 free of charge. Unfortunately, as tourism pres-
sures increase (and so does vandalism and theft), some colleges have
understandably become more reluctant to open their doors, especially
to large parties. Others have started charging for admission. Always
remember you are a guest on private property, don't enter staircases or
rooms unless directed, and be as quiet as possible. If you have any
doubts about admission to a building ask at the gatehouse where the
porters are usually helpful. Large groups must always check in
advance.

Parking: In Oxford there are adjacent multi-storey car parks at the
back of the Westgate shopping centre, Thames St, and smaller, ground-
level car parks at Worcester St, at Hythe Bridge and at St. Clement's St.
The latter is often a good bet. Better still, if you are just in Oxford for
the day leave your car out of town at one of the Park and Ride points
(you will see the road signs or alternatively pick up a leaflet from the
Tourist Information Centre; see **A-Z**). A shuttle bus service operates
every 10-15 min (0720-1830 Mon.-Fri., 0800-1830 Sat., average return
fare 80p) and parking is free.

There are multi-storey car parks at Rother St and Windsor St in Stratford
but the easiest option is to park across the river at Riverside. There is
also ground-level parking at Rother St, at Grove Rd and at Arden St.
Charges vary from 30-40p per hour upwards. Don't waste your time in
either Oxford or Stratford looking for on-street parking.

In the Cotswolds always use the public car parks.

Pitt Rivers Museum, Oxford: This old-fashioned, atmospheric, cluttered museum of ethnography is bursting at the seams with fascinating tribal artefacts from all over the world. Assembled mostly during the 19thC, the most popular items in this Aladdin's cave are the Indian totem poles, the Egyptian mummies, the head-hunting trophies, the awesome collection of killing hardware in the upper gallery and the ornamentally deformed skulls in the lower gallery. You'll never fit it all into one visit but don't worry, it's free, so you can return. There is an annexe, the Balfour building, a 10-min walk away at 60 Banbury Rd (1300-1730 Mon.-Sat. Free), which features primitive musical instruments. You can even hear what they sound like, thanks to a short-wave transmission from the display cases to a set of headphones you are given to wear. See **OXFORD-WHAT TO SEE 2.**

Post Offices: The main offices are at St. Aldate's, Oxford and Bridge St, Stratford. Both open 0900-1730 Mon., Tue., Thu., Fri., 0930-1730 Wed. (staff-training morning), 0900-1230 Sat., and have poste restante facilities. Local post offices may close 1300-1400.

Public Holidays: Most shops and attractions in the area stay open on public holidays, and pubs usually open Sun. hours (see **Opening Times**).
1 Jan. (New Year's Day); Good Friday; Easter Monday; first Mon. in May (May Day); last Mon. in May (Spring Bank Hol.); last Mon. in Aug. (Summer Bank Hol.); 25 Dec. (Christmas Day); 26 Dec. (Boxing Day). If any of the fixed-date holidays fall on a weekend the following Mon. becomes a holiday.

Public Houses: Some of England's best-kept and most attractive pubs can be found in Oxfordshire and the Cotswolds. A typical idyllic hostelry, of which there are many, will be made of rough-hewn golden Cotswold stone, and will feature huge, exposed beams, antique furniture and polished flagstone floors. The newer ones will probably date from the 17thC! The summer focus of attention will probably be the garden, while in the winter a huge log fire will blaze in the large inglenook chimney corner. In recent years pubs have become more

family-conscious, improving their gardens and allowing children into their restaurants. To enter the pub bar or lounge area, however, the law states that children must be aged at least 14, accompanied by an adult and they may not purchase or drink alcohol. A 16-year-old may drink certain alcoholic drinks in the restaurant only. Both of these are subject to the landlord's or landlady's discretion. Alcohol is served only to those aged over 18. See **OXFORD-CITY PUBS**, **OXFORD-COUNTRY PUBS**, **STRATFORD-PUBS**, **Opening Times**.

Punts: See **Boats**.

Railways: Oxford connections from London: hourly departures from Paddington, journey time 65 min. Standard return £19.80, Cheap day return (travel after 1000) £9.80, Awaybreak 5-Day ticket (travel after 0930) £13.20.
Stratford connections: several daily departures from Euston to Coventry, then BR Express coach to Stratford, journey time c.2 hr. Standard return £22.50, child £11.25.
Stratford to Oxford day return £7.20, child £3.60.
Cotswold connections: Paddington to Moreton-in-Marsh via Oxford several times per day, journey time 1hr 45 min. See **Transport**.

Religious Services: Most church denominations are represented in Oxford and Stratford. Churches normally list service times outside their front doors or, alternatively, the TIC (Tourist Information Centre; see **A-Z**) will provide you with a list of churches and times of services.

Royal Shakespeare Theatre (RST): The present theatre, a stark, controversial building best seen from the river, opened in 1932 six years after the original Shakespeare Memorial Theatre was gutted by fire. The Swan Theatre now occupies the shell of the old theatre, built in 1879. The theatre's own permanent company is the Royal Shakespeare Company (RSC), one of the best-known and largest com-

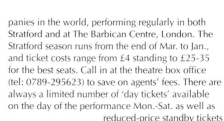

panies in the world, performing regularly in both Stratford and at The Barbican Centre, London. The Stratford season runs from the end of Mar. to Jan., and ticket costs range from £4 standing to £25-35 for the best seats. Call in at the theatre box office (tel: 0789-295623) to save on agents' fees. There are always a limited number of 'day tickets' available on the day of the performance Mon.-Sat. as well as reduced-price standby tickets at £7 available to students and senior citizens. In addition to Shakespeare plays there are lots of other top-quality ad-hoc theatre and music productions.

The third RST theatre, The Other Place, on Southern Lane, stages fringe and contemporary productions and will be re-opened in late 1991. Backstage tours, including the RSC Collection (see **STRATFORD-WHAT TO SEE**), take place 1330, 1530 Mon.-Sat. (except matinée days), 1230, 1415, 1515, 1615 Sun. £2.80, concessions £2. For bookings, tel: 0789-296655. 'After-the-Show' tours are also given punctually after the evening performance, Mon.-Sat. £2. If you want to visit the RST from Oxford, Guide Friday and Spires & Shires both run theatre-service coaches (see **Tours**). See **STRATFORD-WALK**.

Shakespeare, William: William Shakespeare was born on or around 23 April 1564, son of Mary (née Arden) and John, both from farming backgrounds. John was a glove-maker by trade and also took a keen interest in civic affairs. Starting civic office as the borough ale taster, by 1568 he had become bailiff, the town's chief officer. Little is known about his son's childhood but it is thought that he attended the distinguished local grammar school where he would have received a sound education in grammar, logic and rhetoric. Beneath the school is the Guildhall where travelling troupes of actors would have played, and it is likely that this is how young Will would have acquired his first taste for the theatre (especially as his father, in his civic capacity, would have been responsible for entertaining the troupe). At the age of 18 he met Anne Hathaway, got her pregnant and married her. Little is known of Anne and there is not even a surviving likeness of her. Their daughter, Susanna, was born in 1583, and in 1585 twins, Hamnet and Judith, followed. The next significant episode that we know of is that sometime in the late 1580s Shakespeare left Stratford for London. Local legend attributes this to a deer-poaching incident at Charlecote Park (see **STRATFORD-HOUSES, CASTLES & PARKS**), but this is unlikely. There is conjecture that he may have joined one of the troupes of actors who frequently passed through Stratford. The timing was certainly propitious as the theatre was just taking off as an important art form. Shakespeare began as an actor, then became a 'reviser' of plays and finally the play-wright we know. His earliest major work was the historical play *Henry VI, Parts I-III*, 1590-91. He soon drew critical acclaim and *Richard III*, *The Comedy of Errors*, *Titus Andronicus*, *The Taming of the Shrew*, *The Two Gentlemen of Verona* and *Love's Labour's Lost* followed at the rate of two a year until by 1599 he had accumulated enough wealth to become a partner in the Globe Playhouse on London's Bankside. During this time, however, he travelled regularly to and from Stratford (see **OXFORD-WALK 2**) in order to support his family. He also invested his wealth in Stratford, both in business and in property, buying the grandest house in town, New Place, in 1597. He retired here in 1610, wrote his final play, *Henry VIII*, in 1612 and died four years later on his 52nd birthday. He is buried in the parish church of Holy Trinity (see **STRATFORD-WHAT TO SEE**) and his monument, commissioned by his wife,

is the only reliable likeness of 'the Bard of Avon'. Acclaimed as the greatest dramatic genius of the English-speaking peoples, he left a legacy of 34 plays and after nearly 400 years is probably still the most oft-quoted man in the English language. See **STRATFORD-SHAKESPEARE**.

Shakespearean Properties: The five properties most closely associated with Shakespeare are administered by the Shakespeare Birthplace Trust. They have all been impeccably preserved and restored to their original states, each one a picture-postcard view of Tudor England. Each house is staffed by friendly, knowledgeable guides. See **STRATFORD-SHAKESPEARE**, **STRATFORD-WALK**, **Tours**.

Shopping: Oxford is an excellent centre, catering for tourists, a large local population and an international student community (see **OXFORD-SHOPPING**). Stratford is not so well blessed but has many individual shops of character and quality, among them The Tradition of Wales, Henley St; Langman's Fine Cheeses, Wood St; Treasures of Ireland, Sheep St; Waterstone's Bookshop, Bridge St. The best of the modern arcades is the Minories between Meer St and Henley St, while the most interesting browsing is to be had at the delightful Antiques Centre on Ely St, featuring over 50 permanent stalls. Most Cotswold towns and larger villages have antiques and local crafts shops. Antique prices will vary enormously – ask at the TIC (Tourist Information Centre) for venues and dates of local auctions. Most tourist-orientated shops will open Sun. in summer. See **Markets**, **Opening Times**.

The Slaughters: See **OXFORD-EXCURSION 1**.

Snowshill Manor: Without doubt, the Cotswolds' most intriguing collection. A fantastic Aladdin's Cave of craftsmanship from all over the world, spanning four centuries, is crammed into a series of small, atmospherically darkened rooms. Byzantine armour, Oriental cabinets, Tudor furniture, Balinese masks, antique toys, musical instruments and beautiful clocks are a few of the many eclectic treasures. The highlight is The Green Room, featuring a remarkable 'dusk gathering' of 26 Samurai warriors in full armour and battle colours. The adjacent cottage home of Charles Wade, who built up the collection, is equally fascinating and the view from the beautiful terraced gardens across the hills is stunning. Try to avoid summer weekends when the tiny rooms can get uncomfortably crowded. See **STRATFORD-EXCURSION 2**, **Children**.

Sports: Spectator sports in the area are as follows:

Cricket (May-Sep.): The thud of leather on willow and the ripple of polite applause across a village green on Sun. afternoon is as English as you can possibly get. Watch either the University team at the Parks in Oxford, Stratford Cricket Club at Swan's Nest Lane, or any village team.

Football (late Aug.-early May): Oxford United play at home in the Second Division every other Sat. at the Manor Ground, two miles outside the city centre. The nearest First Division team is Coventry City (19 miles from Stratford). Tickets £5-10.

Horse events: The Cheltenham Festival in Mar., with its highlight of the Gold Cup, is one of the premier events in the horse-racing calendar. Other National Hunt meetings also take place regularly at the courses in Stratford and Warwick. Polo matches are held at Cirencester Park on Sun. in summer.

Rowing: Inter-collegiate rivalry to become 'head of the river' is fierce. Eights and Torpids are the big race days (see **Events**).

Rugby union (Sep.-April): This is also enthusiastically embraced by the colleges. Watch them clash at Iffley Rd Sports Centre on Sat. afternoon. The nearest first-class rugby clubs are at Coventry and Cheltenham.

Participator sports which visitors can pursue are as follows:

Fishing: J. Venables & Son, 99 St. Aldate's, Oxford, sells permits for Oxfordshire rivers; A. F. Cooper & Son, 37 Greenhill St, Stratford will sell you permits for the Avon.

Golf: Oxford and the Cotswolds have several clubs which accept visitors. Ask at the TIC (Tourist Information Centre) for a list. The Stratford-upon-Avon Golf Club, tel: 0789-297296, and the Welcombe Hotel Club, tel: 0789-295252, both welcome non-members.

Ice Skating: Oxford has an excellent modern rink on Oxpens Rd (£1.80-£3, tel: 0865-247676).

Sports centres: Oxford has two centres, Stratford has one.

Swimming: Aside from indoor pools at the sports centres there are several outdoor pools in Oxford.

Water sports: The Cotswold Waterpark, one mile west of Fairford (31 miles west of Oxford) offers water-skiing April-Oct., tel: 0285-713735. Linch Hill Leisure Park, Stanton Harcourt (9 miles west of Oxford) has fishing, sailboarding, boating and canoeing, tel: 0865-882215.

For further details of any of these sports contact the TIC (Tourist Information Centre; see **A–Z**).

Stow-on-the-Wold: 21 miles from Stratford, 27 miles from Oxford. Pop: 1900. Everything of interest lies around the large, elegant square in this handsome market town. The Market Hall, built in 1878, effectively divides it in two. In front, a small part of the old green, complete with stocks (where wrong-doers were left to the rough justice of the mob), still survives. Behind is a medieval cross and the church. The shops, galleries and pubs around the square date mostly from the 17th and 18thC. If you like dolls or teddy bears don't miss Lillian Middleton's shops on Sheep St. The TIC (Tourist Information Centre) is at Talbot Court, off the square. See **OXFORD-EXCURSION 1**.

Stratford-upon-Avon: 40 miles north of Oxford. Pop: 21,000. It is often said that but for one man, Stratford would be just another attractive market town in the heart of England. Of course, it is inextricably linked with William Shakespeare (see **A–Z**) but its riverside views and recreation, its beautiful Tudor buildings and the lovely Old Town area make it well worth any tourist's while regardless of their interest in the Bard. The Birthplace and Anne Hathaway's Cottage each attract over half a million visitors every year, making Stratford one of England's biggest provincial draws. At the height of the tourist season, the five small houses which comprise the Shakespearean Properties (see **STRATFORD-SHAKESPEARE**, **A–Z**) come under relentless siege but at other times of the year Stratford hustles and bustles without ever really disturbing the serenity which its location and history have bestowed upon it. Allow around two days to explore the town and all its attractions but with the north Cotswolds and Warwick so close, this a good base for a week or more.

Sudeley Castle: Winchcombe, 22 miles south of Stratford. Although this is not a fortress in the Warwick mould (see **Warwick Castle**), Sudeley is nevertheless a grand castle. Originally built in the 15thC, it was effectively destroyed in 1643 in the Civil War (1642-48) as a result of its being a Royalist stronghold, and it lay in ruins until its

19thC restoration by the Dent-Brocklehurst family. The castle has had strong royal associations for centuries and Henry VIII and three of his wives have all left their mark here. Katherine Parr, Henry's last wife, moved into Sudeley on the King's death in 1548, but within a year she too had died and she is buried here. The apartments are royally appointed and contain masterpieces by Turner, Rubens, Van Dyck and Constable. The formal gardens are in contrast with the beautiful open countryside and there is a good waterfowl collection. Craftsmen may be seen at work in the castle.

Visitors to Sudeley should remember that there are many other attractions to be enjoyed in and around the town of Winchcombe (see **A-Z**). See **STRATFORD-EXCURSION 1**.

Taxis: Cabs can be hailed on the street if they have an illuminated *For Hire* sign showing, or from a rank or by phone. If you intend to call a cab by phone in Oxford to catch a bus or train connection, be sure to leave plenty of time – phone the taxi-cab company at least 40 min before you want to arrive at the station. You may have to 'phone the company more than once to get your cab to turn up.

The central rank in Oxford is at St. Giles and in Stratford at Rother St, Bridge St and at Bridge Foot. Taxis also wait at the railway stations. The standard metered rate is £1.40 for the first mile and 80p per mile after that (there is a 50% surcharge on Sun., bank hol. and after 2400). Minicabs are generally not metered and you should establish the fare before setting off. These can be cheaper than metered cabs over longer distances but they cannot be hailed on the street. See **Transport**.

Theatre: The main theatre in Oxford is The Apollo, George St, which features all aspects of the mainstream performing arts. The principal fringe venue is the Burton Taylor Studio Theatre (behind The Oxford Playhouse, off Gloucester Green) which divides between student drama and professional fringe touring companies. The Newman Rooms, St. Aldate's and the Oxford Union (Mayfly Theatre) at St. Michael's St (off Cornmarket St) also stage student productions. The Pegasus at Magdalen Rd (off Iffley Rd) is the home of the Oxford Youth Theatre who produce fringe and experimental plays. Other venues include The

Old Fire Station Studio Theatre and the Oxford Playhouse, where actors such as Richard Burton once debuted (due to reopen in late 1991). Tickets for all these theatres cost around £5-6 (although The Apollo costs more) and can be bought from Tickets in Oxford at the TIC (Tourist Information Centre; see **A-Z**) in St. Aldate's. The Chipping Norton Theatre also has a lively programme of theatre, opera, music and film. For theatre in Stratford, see **Royal Shakespeare Theatre**.

Tourist Information: The main TIC (Tourist Information Centre) in
Oxford is at St. Aldate's (0930-1700 Mon.-Sat., tel: 0865-726871). In
Stratford it is at Bridge Foot (same hours). Guide Friday (see **Guides**,
Tours) have their own information centres at the railway station in
Oxford (0900-1930 April-Oct., 0900-1600/1800 Nov.-Mar., tel: 0865-
790522) and the Civic Hall, Rother St, Stratford (0830-1900 April-Oct.,
0900-1730 Nov.-Mar., tel: 0789-294466). There are also TICs in some
of the more popular Cotswold towns and villages (see individual town
listings). Opening hours are normally 0900-1700 Mon.-Sat., with
extended hours and Sun. opening in summer. They will give you
general advice on where to go, sell you maps and are a good place to
pick up leaflets, etc. All the major centres also offer accommodation-
booking services (Guide Friday charge £2 per reservation. Oxford TIC
charge £2 plus a refundable deposit and Stratford TIC charge 10% of
room rate). See **Guides**, **Orientation**, **Tours**, **What's On**.

Tours: Guide Friday run an open-top bus tour around Oxford city
with free reboarding at any point. Tours are every 30 min and the complete tour lasts 1 hr (£4, senior citizen £3, child 5-12 £1.50). Tickets are
available from Guide Friday at the railway station or TIC (Tourist Information Centre). The Oxford Classic Tour do exactly the same service
for the same prices and you buy your ticket on the bus. Spires & Shires
do several full-day trips around the Cotswolds, including Blenheim
Palace (see **A-Z**), North Oxfordshire and Vale of the White Horse (£20-
£25 per person inclusive of lunch, cream tea and admission charges).
Their evening tours go to country pubs (depart 2000, £5 transport only).
Both Whites of Oxford and the Oxford & Cotswold Tour Co. do person-
alized tours and Whites also run regular Cotswolds village tours.
Guide Friday run an open-top bus tour around Stratford and to Mary
Arden's and Anne Hathaway's properties (see **STRATFORD-SHAKESPEARE**,
Shakespearean Properties). Tours are every 15-30 min, with free
reboarding at any point (£3.50, senior citizens £3, child 5-12 £1.50;
this fee entitles the holder to a special ticket to any three of the
Shakespearean Properties for £4). Buy your ticket from Guide Friday
office, Rother St, or on the bus.
In the Cotswolds, Guide Friday do the following tours (from Stratford):

'The Cotswold Tour', lasting 4 hr, in a vintage single-decker bus calling at various destinations (£10, child 5-12 £5); 'The Cotswold Evening Tour', visiting pubs in the area (1900 May-Aug. £10); and 'The Blenheim Palace Tour' to Bladon church (Churchill's grave), Woodstock (see **A-Z**) and Blenheim Palace (£10, child 5-12 £5; this fee entitles the holder to discount on admission to the Palace). Guide Friday also do a tour from Stratford to Warwick via Charlecote House (see **STRATFORD-HOUSES, CASTLES & PARKS**) and Kenilworth Castle (see **STRATFORD-HOUSES, CASTLES & PARKS**) with photo-stops only (£7, child 5-12 £3.50; this fee entitles the holder to discount on admission to Warwick Castle; see **A-Z**).
Tickets and times for all these tours are available from the TIC (Tourist Information Centre; see **A-Z**) or from the tour companies themselves. See **Guides**.

Transport: If you plan on staying just in Oxford or Stratford for the duration of your stay you may be better off saving expensive car-hire charges and using organized tours to see the countryside and public transport to see other towns. If you want to see more of the Cotswolds, however, a car is necessary. See **Buses**, **Railways**, **Taxis**.

Walks: There are several short, countrified walks around Oxford town centre (see **OXFORD-WALK 3**, **Christ Church College, Oxford**, **Magdalen College, Oxford**). The University Parks make for a very pleasant stroll: over to the Rainbow Bridge by the Cherwell, across to the duckpond and back to watch the cricket (Sun.). Another short walk is across Christ Church Meadow to the Botanic Gardens (see **OXFORD-WHAT TO SEE 1**). In Stratford the walks to Anne Hathaway's Cottage (start from Grove Rd, behind Rother St) and to Mary Arden's House (follow the canal off the Birmingham Rd.) are both pleasurable.
The Cotswolds are a mecca for serious walkers with the 100-mile-long Cotswold Way footpath the biggest challenge. Footpaths are clearly marked and every local TIC (Tourist Information Centre) stocks a plethora of walking guidebooks and maps (the Ordnance Survey 1:50,000 map is recommended). If you are not sure whether you are the independent-walking type, why not join a Cotswold warden for a guided walk (see **Guides**).

Warwick: 8 miles northeast of Stratford. Pop: 22,000. Market day Sat. It would be a shame if the only thing you saw in Warwick was the castle (see **Warwick Castle**), particularly as its other attractions are so close. The two 'musts' are St. Mary's church, Church St (0900-1800 summer, 0900-1600 winter) and the Lord Leycester (pronounced 'Leicester') Hospital, High St (1000-1730 Mon.-Sat., summer; 1000-1630 Mon.-Sat., winter. £1.50, concessions £1, child 50p). The church includes the splendid 15thC Beauchamp Chapel, built for the powerful Dudley family (who owned Warwick Castle) and includes a monument to Robert Dudley, favourite of Elizabeth I. In 1571 he founded the Lord Leycester Hospital as an asylum for his aged and infirm servants. Its picturesque buildings are remarkable survivors and the hospital's Brethren's Kitchen is a friendly, atmospheric spot for tea or lunch. The TIC (Tourist Information Centre) is on Jury St. See **Tours**.

Warwick Castle: Superlatives are heaped on Warwick and it is undoubtedly one of Britain's finest castles. From the top of its awesome 14thC towers with their marvellous, commanding views, to the bowels of its dank dungeons, you cannot help but feel a dramatic sense of history here. The armoury and the magnificent Great Hall and State Rooms are particularly memorable. Madame Tussaud's also do an excellent job, recreating a 'Royal weekend party' which was held at the castle in 1898. The grounds are superb and are ideal for a picnic. Allow half a day here. See **STRATFORD-HOUSES, CASTLES & PARKS**, **Tours**.

What's On: *The Oxford Times* is Oxford's main daily newspaper. *This Month in Oxford* is a free events-listing booklet available at various outlets in the city. There is a monthly day-by-day information guide on sale for 70p and an information sheet is posted in shops, pubs, libraries, etc. daily in term time and weekly during vacations. In Stratford *The Herald* (published on Fri.) is the main listings source but you should also look in the *Stratford Evening Telegraph*. If you want to know what's happening in Birmingham, pick up *What's On Birmingham* – you may get a free copy from the TIC (Tourist Information Centre) at Bridge Foot. See **Events**.

Winchcombe: 22 miles south of Stratford. Pop: 6000. This charming, small town is remarkably unaffected by tourism, given its size and location. The garden of the Old Bakery Tea Shoppe – one of the best tearooms in the Cotswolds – is a fine place to appreciate Winchcombe's valley setting in a fold of the hills. The church is in the best 'wool church' traditions (see **Wool**): large and perpendicular-style, with fine monuments. Don't miss its splendid grotesques and gargoyles (see **A-Z**). To the left of the High St are the pretty, 19thC Sudeley Almshouses in Dent St and close by in Vineyard St are more tiny, delightful cottages. The Winchcombe Railway Museum is a little further on (1330-1800 Easter-Oct., 1330-dusk Sat., Sun. only winter. £1.40, accompanied child under 16 30p). This extensive and evocative collection of railway relics and memorabilia is laid out around a pretty garden complete with a pets' corner for children, and will charm even non-railway fans (see **Children**). Try the Old Corner Cupboard for lunch. The Folk and Police Museum is in the Town Hall (1000-1230, 1400-1630 Mon.-Sat., April-Oct. 50p, concessions and child 30p, family £1). The TIC (Tourist Information Centre) is also located here. See STRATFORD-EXCURSION 1, **Sudeley Castle**.

Witney: 12 miles west of Oxford. Pop: 18,000. Market days Thu., Sat. The centre of this Cotswold market town is marked by its ancient Buttercross, dating back to at least the 17thC. Sheep were bought and sold here until 1950 and the town has been famous for its blankets for centuries (see **Wool**). Blankets are still finished (though no longer woven) in Witney and you can see the elegant Blanket Weaver's Hall (built 1721), with its unusual one-handed clock, towards the far end of the High St. Almost opposite is Peace & Co., selling Witney blankets, and near to them is Ian Pont Antiques featuring a small teddy bear museum. Going out of town is Early's, Witney's last surviving mill, where visits are sometimes allowed (ask at the Tourist Information Centre situated in the ancient Town Hall, opposite the Buttercross). Stroll across the lovely green to see the parish church which dates from the 12th-15thC. For refreshments try The Angel by the Buttercross or the 16thC Royal Oak on High St. See OXFORD-EXCURSION 2.

The stocks at Woodstock

Woodstock: 8 miles northwest of Oxford. Pop: 2000. This elegant, compact market town is mostly used by tourists as the 'side door' to Blenheim Palace (see **A-Z**) but it deserves to be explored in its own right. Its facade is Georgian but the fabric of many Woodstock properties is at least a century older than that. Visit the Oxfordshire County Museum (1000-1600 Tue.-Fri., 1000-1700 Sat., 1400-1700 Sun. Free) for the history of the county, with the emphasis on rural and agricultural life. Woodstock has a long tradition of glove-making, and this is still carried on today in Chaucer Lane. The best place for lunch is the excellent garden bar of The Feathers. The TIC (Tourist Information Centre) is open in summer only and is at Hensington Rd (off A34). See **OXFORD-EXCURSION 1**, **Events**, **Tours**.

Wool: 'In Europe the best wool is English, in England the best wool is Cotswold', ran a line from a medieval song. Cotswold wool tax was used to pay the ransom of Richard I, the Lion-Heart (quite appropriately, as the huge, shaggy sheep are known as Cotswold Lions) and even today the Lord Chancellor of England sits on a woolsack to remind us of how great a commodity wool once was to England. The Cotswold Lion is an ancient breed, still the largest and bearing the heaviest fleece of any British sheep. Their heyday was in early medieval times and a single abbey might own a flock of 500,000 alone. The early-18thC author Daniel Defoe recorded 90,000 sheep sold in a single day at Stow-on-the-Wold long after the woollen trade had peaked. Changing farming methods, overtaxation and the growth of a home-based weaving trade killed off the export trade, and due to the declining demand for wool this century the Cotswold Lion even faced extinction in the 1930s. The breed is now expanding again and new flocks are being set up. The legacy of the great days can be seen in the 'wool churches' all over the Cotswolds, and in various other great buildings (see **Winchcombe**). The best place to see Cotswold wool in use today is at the Cotswold Woollen Weavers in Filkins (see OXFORD-EXCURSION 2), while if you want to see the Cotswold Lions go to Cogges Manor Farm Museum (see OXFORD-HOUSES & PARKS), Broadway Tower Country Park (see STRATFORD-EXCURSION 2) or the Cotswold Farm Park (see STRATFORD-EXCURSION 1). See **Cotswolds**.

Youth Hostels: In Oxford there is a hostel at Jack Straw's Lane, Headington: take a no. 73 bus from St. Aldate's (Feb.-Nov., closed for one month in either Dec. or Jan., and Sun. in Feb. and Nov. Bed only £3.50-5, tel: 0865-62997). In Stratford go to Hemingford House, Alveston, two miles from the town (Mar.-Jan. Bed and breakfast £6-8, tel: 0789-297093). There are also hostels at Stow-on-the-Wold (see **A-Z**) in Market Sq., and at Charlbury, 7 miles from Chipping Norton. If you're not a member of the YHA (Youth Hostels Association) you can join at any hostel (£1.70 under 16, £4 16-20, £7.60 for over 21s). There is a YWCA hostel at Alexandra Residential Club, 133 Woodstock Rd, Oxford, but accommodation is usually available only in July and Aug. (Bed only £6-16, tel: 0865-52021).